INSIGHTS
ON POLICY

ADDITIONAL WORKS BY THE AUTHOR

BOOKS

How to Manage in Times of Crisis, 2009

The Ideal Executive: Why You Cannot Be One and What to Do About It,
LEADERSHIP TRILOGY, VOL. 1, 2004

*Management/Mismanagement Styles: How to Identify a Style
and What to Do About It,* LEADERSHIP TRILOGY, VOL. 2, 2004

*Leading the Leaders: How to Enrich Your Style of Management and Handle People
Whose Style is Different From Yours*, LEADERSHIP TRILOGY, VOL. 3, 2004

*Managing Corporate Lifecycles: An Updated and Expanded Look
at the Classic Work,* Corporate Lifecycles, 2004

The Pursuit of Prime, 1996

Mastering Change: The Power of Mutual Trust and Respect, 1992

*Corporate Lifecycles: How and Why Corporations Grow and Die
and What to Do About It*, 1988

How to Solve the Mismanagement Crisis, 1979

Self-Management: New Dimensions to Democracy.
With Elisabeth M. Borgese, 1975

Industrial Democracy: Yugoslav Style, 1971

BOTTOM-LINE MANAGEMENT EXCERPTS VIDEO SERIES

1. *How to Define an Organization's Mission* (18:33 min.)
2. *What is First: Strategy or Structure?* (23:24 min.)
3. *The Signs of Organizational Aging* (13:09 min.)
4. *From Entrepreneurship to Professional Management* (24:32 min.)
5. *Management and Mismanagement Styles* (32:40 min.)
6. *How to Hire the Right People* (21:25 min.)
7. *How to Delegate* (13:38 min.)
8. *The Ideal Executive* (19:06 min.)
9. *What Is a Leader?* (16:33 min.)
10. *The Secret of Success of Any Organization* (25:36 min.)

To place an order or see a full list of Adizes publications, visit
www.adizes.com/store.

INSIGHTS
ON POLICY

ICHAK KALDERON ADIZES
Founder, Adizes Institute
Santa Barbara, California

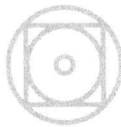

Library of Congress Cataloging-in-Publication Data

Adizes, Ichak.
Insights on Policy

ISBN: 978-0-937120-12-5

Library of Congress Control Number Pending

Published by
Adizes Institute Publications
1212 Mark Avenue
Carpinteria
Santa Barbara County, California, USA 93013
805-565-2901; Fax 805-565-0741
Website: www.adizes.com

Design and layout by RJ Communications LLC, New York
Printed in the United States of America

Additional copies may be ordered from:
www.adizes.com/store

To my friend and colleague
Carlos Valdesuso
on his 70th birthday,
in celebration of thirty years of
friendship and collaboration

CONTENTS

INTRODUCTION

T HE Adizes blog, which is posted at least once a week on the Adizes Institute website (http://www.adizes.com/blog) and sent by e-mail to thousands of subscribers, began life in 2003 as a monthly column called "Insights."

They were, literally, *insights*, rather than the products of scientific research. I dared to say what I thought. In doing so, I opened myself up to criticism.

And that is what I got: Many people wrote to say they disagreed with one or more of my observations or conclusions. But they kept reading, because what I wrote made them think. Which is exactly what I set out to achieve.

Recently, I decided to publish the essays in book form. I cherish books; I suppose in that way I will always belong to the pre-Internet generation. The Internet, blogs, and tweets are great for speed and mass distribution, but to me they seem temporary, perishable, while a book has permanency.

In this book—the first of a series of Insights collections—all of the essays deal with governmental policy, both within and among nations. The ideas for the Insights column often evolved out of something I saw or heard or felt as I traveled around the world, consulting to organizations that included government administrations, Parliaments, Cabinets, and sometimes even the president of the country.

Then, in light of the response from my readers, I often rethought the essays, re-edited or rewrote them, and also updated the ones that needed it.

So here, in that somewhat changed form, are my thoughts as they evolved at the beginning of the 21st century, as I witnessed changes—as well as their unintended consequences—occurring before my own eyes.

In particular, these Insights offer a fascinating close-up of how countries all over the world—developed countries as well as countries in transition— dealt first with the phenomenon of globalization, and then recently with a Western financial crisis that went viral within hours, proving a point that I have often tried to make: that, like it or not, countries are going to have to learn to live and work together, or they are not likely to survive well.

Some of my observations, even those written less than five years ago, might appear outdated, even antiquated. But that, too, is a valuable observation: If my opinion seems quaint only three years after I wrote it, that is even more proof (as if we needed more proof) that change is accelerating beyond the capacity of human beings to deal with it reasonably.

I hope these Insights will stir debate.

I want to take this opportunity to thank my editor, Nan Goldberg, whose editing helped me sharpen my thinking.

–Ichak Kalderon Adizes, Ph.D.

PART 1

GLOBAL CHALLENGES IN LEADING CHANGE

Discussing What Matters[1]

W E are rapidly approaching a crossroads that will determine whether or not our civilization has a future. Depending on what we do, we could face either total apocalypse or a new Age of Aquarius. We could experience an exciting new culture, our behavior dominated by mutual trust and respect, or a complete destruction of civilization.

Allow me to elaborate.

The Repercussions of Change

We know that change is constant. The process of change has been going on since the beginning of time and will continue forever. Among other factors, the world is changing physically, technologically, socially, and economically.

Change is not only here to stay, it is also accelerating. More scientists are alive today than accumulatively throughout the history of mankind.

While change, on one hand, brings advances in standards of living and even in our life span, it also causes stress and disintegration, which are manifested in what we call "problems." And problems, when not resolved in a timely manner, grow to become crises.

How Change Creates Problems

To explain how change causes disintegration, let me begin with a premise: Everything is part of some kind of a system, and every system is a sub-system of some larger system.

Systems and sub-systems, which interrelate, do not necessarily change at the same rate; some change faster than others.

Take human beings, for example. Everyone is composed of many

---

[1] Speech, given January 22, 2010 at Corvinus University, Budapest, Hungary, on the occasion of being awarded a Doctor Honoris Causa degree; published in The Journal of Corvinus University of Budapest, Society and Economy, Vol. 32 No. 2, December 2010.

sub-systems, among them the physiological, the intellectual, the emotional, and the spiritual. They do not necessarily develop in synchronicity. And when sub-systems do not change in synchronicity, gaps occur that destroy the unity, or integrity, of the system.

For instance, a person might be 40 years old chronologically, but still be a teenager emotionally; physically, she might feel 60 years old, and yet spiritually not even be born. We would say that this person does not "have it together."

> *Conflict is like rushing water. It creates energy, which, if harnessed, creates electricity. If not harnessed, it becomes a destructive flood.*

On a corporate level, sub-systems also change at different rates. For instance, in a young, growing company, marketing and sales change rapidly, while the accounting system changes very slowly. The outcome, again, is disintegration, manifested in the problem of lack of information: Management increasingly does not know what is happening.

On a macro level, we also experience disintegrating forces of change. Right now, we are in the midst of a "third wave" of transformation.[2] The "first wave" was the transition from a nomadic to an agricultural, or agrarian, society; the "second wave" was the Industrial Revolution, which caused urbanization that was accompanied by urban blight, congestion, and the dehumanization of labor, among other manifestations.

Now, we are experiencing a "third wave"—also known as the "post-industrial," the "information," or the "knowledge" economy—accompanied by a new set of problems: Those who are unable to adapt to the changes become unemployed, economically disadvantaged, or left behind in some other way. I suggest that crime, for instance, is a manifestation of economic, political, social, or psychological disintegration caused by change. The same applies to homelessness. And I believe you would find a significant correlation between the rate of divorce and the rate of change in a given geographic location.

Change is constant. Change causes disintegration, manifested in what we

---

[2] Alvin Toffler, in his influential books *The Third Wave* (Bantam, 1980) and its sequel, *Powershift* (Bantam, 1990), presented his "wave" theory of societies, predicting that the "third wave" would be characterized by the eclipse of manufacturing by information processing as a determinant of power and wealth; a trend away from consensus and standardization; the rise of regional and separatist movements; and an assault on the nation-state by non-national entities such as multinational corporations, religions with global reach, and organizations such as the European Union, NAFTA, and the International Criminal Court.

call "problems"—which, if not treated in a timely manner, will eventually evolve into a crisis.

If you analyze any problem you might have—with your car, your marriage, your career—you will find that something has fallen apart, and it has fallen apart because of change. But that is not the whole story.

On Being Interconnected

Change is not only a centrifugal, disintegrating force, but also a centripetal force. While we are disintegrating on one hand, we are also becoming more interdependent than ever before: the Internet, air travel, television, world banking interdependencies, etc., are turning the world into a "global village."

We can see those centripetal forces in the social sciences: Since the 1980s, teaching and research have become increasingly interdisciplinary.[3] Degrees are offered in the relatively new fields of neuroscience, biochemistry, and geobiology. It is no longer possible to make economic policy while ignoring political and social repercussions. This overlap of fields, disciplines, and bodies of knowledge is even reflected in the phenomenon of unisex fashion.

This centripetal force means that a problem in one part of the world, caused by local disintegration, can rapidly migrate beyond the borders of a country, unaffected by mere political or even physical boundaries, to become systemic in nature and even global in span. At that point, it is far more intense, more complicated, and less likely to be solved without global cooperation, which is difficult to mobilize. The swine flu and the credit crisis of 2008-2009 are two examples of crises that began locally and quickly became global and systemic, affecting multiple systems—the economy, the culture—and creating political repercussions.

Solutions > Diversity > Conflict

Problems and crises call for decision-making to reach a solution. And solutions have their own consequences: They generate conflicts, because

---

[3] Julie Thompson Klein, *Crossing Boundaries: Knowledge, Disciplinaries, and Interdisciplinarities* (University Press of Virginia, 1996).

people have different opinions about what the solution should be. For instance, political liberals and conservatives believe in different—often opposite—solutions to problems.

In addition, people have a diversity of self-interests. A solution that satisfies one person's interests might adversely affect the interests of others.

Thus, the more problems there are, the more solutions are called for. The more solutions are being sought, the more conflict there will be.

Conclusion: The more change we experience, the more conflict we will have.

And the more conflict, the more stress.

There is a well-known psychological test that assigns points to various life events.[4] For instance, losing your job means so many points; death in the family, more points. Even going on vacation has points. The common denominator? Change.

It is not news to anyone that the more developed the nation, the faster is the rate of change, the more stressed people are, and the more prevalent are the psychological problems that such stress causes.

To avoid this stress, people—and nations—often choose *not* to solve a problem. For them, a conflict may seem potentially more painful than living with the problem that needs a solution.

But deciding not to solve a problem is also a decision: a decision to do nothing. And that might be the worst decision we could possibly make. Unfortunately, doing nothing does not mean that change will stop and that the problem will freeze in one place or at the same level of magnitude. While we do nothing, the world will keep changing and the problem will keep intensifying. Continuous change will cause continuous disintegration; if the accompanying problems are not treated, they will eventually become a crisis—and doing nothing will no longer be an option.

CONFLICTS ARE INEVITABLE

We need to understand that conflicts will continue to arise forever, out of the need to solve problems that are caused by change. The only way to avoid having conflicts is not to have problems. But we can stop having problems

---

[4] The Holmes and Rahe Stress Scale (SRRS); see T.H. Holmes and R.H. Rahe, "The social readjustments rating scales," *Journal of Psychosomatic Research*, 11:213-218, 1967.

only if we stop change—and that can only happen when the system is dead. Life means change, and change means problems, and problems call for solutions, which means gathering different opinions and affecting different interests—which generates conflicts.

Conflict is the nature of change, which is the nature of life.

The sequence of the reasoning is:

Change ＞ disintegration > problems > require solutions > diversity of opinions, judgments, and interests > conflicts

ARE WARS ALSO INEVITABLE?

Change, problems, diversity, and conflicts are inevitable. They are life.

If change cannot be stopped, and thus conflict cannot be eliminated, does that mean that wars, destruction, annihilation, and Armageddon are unavoidable?

We all know that conflict can be destructive. It destroys marriages, companies, and countries.

The bad news is that modern conflicts can have major repercussions and could potentially be fatal to mankind. In the modern world, technology has now made possible the destruction of our entire civilization. We have nuclear capabilities and the power to destroy ourselves at a magnitude previously unknown to human beings, while our values and behavior have barely progressed since the Stone Age: We still try to kill those who threaten us, even though sometimes the perceived "threat" consists of simply having different religious or political beliefs.

> I subscribe to Emanuel Kant's definition of respect: to recognize the sovereignty of the other party to think differently.

Consequently, in the past century human beings have slaughtered each other on a scale previously unimaginable. The ferocity of the 1990s conflict in the Balkans—where Europeans, with their supposedly enlightened culture and widespread education, nevertheless behaved like savages—is graphic evidence of the fate we may be heading toward.

Clearly, such destructive conflict has become untenable.

Are we doomed?

No, not all is lost. Conflict can be constructive, too.

Look at Switzerland, which is composed of several ethnic groups—the Germans, the French, and the Italians—that have been at each other's throats since before the First World War. Switzerland should long ago have destroyed itself from within. But that has not happened.

And we all know of some marriages in which the partners are different in style and outlook, that somehow do not end in divorce. In fact, some of them seem to bond even closer together—not in spite of, but because of their differences.

Conflict is like rushing water. It creates energy, which, if harnessed, creates electricity. If not harnessed, it becomes a destructive flood.

Remember the rule of entropy,[5] which dictates that if we do not act to prevent it, diversity will naturally tilt us toward the path of destabilization and destruction.

We need to take our destiny in our hands. We need to act. And act correctly.

MARX'S ATTEMPT TO ELIMINATE CONFLICT

Karl Marx lived and wrote during the Industrial Revolution in Europe and witnessed the conflicts that changes brought. To avoid those conflicts and their accompanying pain, he prescribed a "dictatorship of the proletariat"; by "dictatorship," he meant there would be only one political party. Thus, his system permitted only one opinion, one point of view. Naturally, that should have eliminated conflicts in decision-making.

Under Marx's Communist system, there were to be no conflicts of interests, either. In a classless society, organized around the principle "from each according to his ability, to each according to his need," everyone's interests would be the same.[6]

---

[5] The theory of entropy, also known as the 2nd Law of Thermodynamics, states that any closed system naturally tends to move away from a state of order (low entropy) to a state of maximum disorder (high entropy). Movement toward order requires energy, whereas a system's spontaneous movement over time will always tend toward increasing disorder and disintegration.

[6] Karl Marx, *Critique of the Gotha Programme*. Marx/Engels Selected Works, Vol. 3, p. 13-30, written in 1875 (Moscow: Progress Publishers, 1970). It was in this document that Marx used the phrases famously associated with him, predicting a "dictatorship of the proletariat" and summarizing his philosophy as "from each according to his ability, to each according to his need." See also *The Communist Manifesto*, written with Friedrich Engels and first published in German in 1848.

In fact, Marx argued, when perfect Communism was attained, there would be no more conflict at all, and happiness would rule on earth.

So what happened?

In order to stop conflicts, you have to stop change.

When Marxism was applied, change stopped. The Soviet Union's art and industry remained frozen in the 19th century. Innovation became virtually non-existent, except in the scientific and military fields.

While Marx's diagnosis of society had relevance, his prescription was a disaster.

No one in the history of mankind has succeeded in stopping change over time. Thus, conflicts cannot be stopped, either.

PICCO'S THEORY OF DIVERSITY

It was Dr. Gianni Picco, a former United Nations assistant secretary-general for political affairs, who helped me realize that the prevailing conflict of the 21st century is between those that support diversity (democratic regimes) and those that oppose it (Fascism, Communism, and fanatical religious movements, of which Muslim extremists are currently the largest and most vocal).

Both groups continually face problems caused by change. The anti-diversity group tries to eradicate the problems that change generates by trying to stop change altogether, while the other side favors accelerated change and struggles to find ways to support and protect diversity and make conflict constructive rather than destructive.

This confrontation between pro-diversity and anti-diversity regimes is not a new phenomenon. It can be traced, in various forms, back through the centuries. It has had numerous manifestations, from the struggle between Athens and Sparta to World War II, when the totalitarian governments of Germany, Japan, and Italy aligned themselves as an Axis against the United States, Great Britain, and the other liberal Allies. Today, the story is repeating itself, with radical Muslims replacing Fascists as enemies of democracy.

DIVERSITY CANNOT BE PREVENTED

Opposing diversity is and always has been a utopian effort, doomed to failure, because the only way to stop diversity is to stop change. And change cannot be stopped, only retarded. Problems caused by change cannot be eliminated, only postponed. Eventually, those problems will have to be dealt with, and any solution will reveal significant differences of opinion and judgment and affect a variety of interests.

Even when diversity is suppressed, over time it will re-emerge—because people change. No one remains frozen in the same attitude, with the same experiences and the same beliefs, forever. Even within the Communist party there were differences of opinion.[7] The same is true of today's radical Muslims—or any other radicals who oppose diversity, for that matter. Radicals, by definition, cannot bear compromise; thus if those who insist on clubbing diversity to death ever stop battling the West, they are likely to turn on each other, finding heresy in smaller and smaller disparities.

No amount of force can eradicate diversity. In fact, the harder radical groups fight to eliminate diversity, the more acute the conflict becomes. In trying to stop diversity, we do not achieve peace. On the contrary, we only create more misery.

LEARNING TO CAPITALIZE ON DIVERSITY

If diversity is inevitable and eternal, how should we deal with the conflicts that result?

Let me repeat: The answer is not to prohibit diversity or find ways to minimize it. These are utopian measures that do not and cannot work.

Instead, we must develop policies and mechanisms that convert conflict to a constructive, rather than destructive, force.

Some countries already have such a system in place; it's called democracy. But even when it is long-established and effective, democracies have yet to transcend the national level: While democratic states forbid murdering those who disagree with them inside their own borders, for example, they continue to applaud the notion of murdering those of other nationalities who differ from them. They even make heroes of those who kill the most.

Internationally, we have neither the political platform through which

---

[7] Robert Service, *Trotsky: A Biography* (Harvard University Press, 2009). One example: Leon Trotsky, a leading architect of the 1917 Russian Revolution, was forced into exile in 1929 for opposing Stalin's policy of achieving "socialism in one country" first—a shocking deviation from established Communist theory, which called for a simultaneous, international "permanent revolution." Stalin had Trotsky assassinated in Mexico in 1940.

global differences can be resolved and solutions reached and implemented, nor the know-how to mobilize that platform. What we do have—the United Nations—is a forum where individual states represent their own individual interests. It is not a pl atform for governing the global interests of Mother Earth.

I suggest that we must learn—and quickly—how to convert the natural and to-be-expected conflicts that diversity brings into a constructive force. It is the only option.

But how?

MUTUAL TRUST AND RESPECT

What determines whether or not a conflict can be constructive is not whether conflict exists, but how it is handled. We have to learn how to handle conflict constructively—which is to say, to handle diversity constructively.

My forty years of clinical work with companies have shown me that conflict can be constructive (as opposed to destructive) only when there is mutual trust and respect.

Mutual trust and respect is the methodology for healing disintegration that is caused by change.

If change causes disintegration, manifested by what we call problems, then it follows that the antidote to this "illness" is integration, or healing: making whole. Mutual trust and respect are the integrative tools with which to achieve that.

We need a culture of mutual trust and respect on a global level.

Allow me to elaborate.

THE MEANING OF 'RESPECT'

I subscribe to Emanuel Kant's definition of respect: to recognize the sovereignty of the other party to think differently. When such an attitude prevails, we are open to learning from people's disagreements. There is not much to learn from people who agree with us, because all their agreement does is reinforce our previously held opinions. When we learn from those who disagree with us, we enrich ourselves with information we did not have. Thus we make better decisions. The result is that we learn to value their disagreement.

In Hebrew, the word for "respect" has two meanings: "to honor" and "to value." Honoring, to me, is ritualistic, while "to value" a difference of opinion is functional. I use the word "respect" in the second sense, meaning "to value" someone. That happens when we allow ourselves to learn from the differences that someone manifests in his or her opinions.

Mutual respect is a necessary component of learning and thus of enriching ourselves with information we did not have; you can't learn from people you don't respect. The famous remark generally attributed to Voltaire, "I disapprove of what you say, but I'll defend to the death your right to say it,"[8] demonstrates the kind of respect that democracy is based on: respect for differences of opinion, and legal protection for those who think differently.

On a global scale, mutual respect means to respect different cultures. It means to seek what we can learn from those who are different from us. The Hindu culture can teach us the value of surrendering, of meditation and yoga; the Protestant culture, the value of work; the Jewish culture, the value of education; etc. Some cultures are looked down upon as being inferior, of lower value—the Gypsies, for instance. But there are valuable lessons to be learned from Gypsy culture, too: They truly live in the moment and enjoy life with an unparalleled passion.

Every culture offers something unique to the totality of humankind.

The same applies to political diversity. Conservatives have a different point of view than liberals. Much can be learned from both. Every point of view potentially carries some value.

Can we value differences? We must. Without mutual respect, we are constantly at war. With it, we continue to grow in our understanding and enrich our lives as well.

THE MEANING OF 'TRUST'

Trust is different from respect. Trust occurs when there is a shared belief that a commonality of interests exists, and that the future will be better for everyone, not just one group. Without that faith, people fear that some will benefit more than others, and that the sacrifices of one group will not be shared by the others—that in transactions between groups, one group will

---

[8] In fact, the aphorism cannot be found in Voltaire's writings. It first appeared in a book called *Friends of Voltaire*, by S.G. Tallentyre (1906), and was intended to paraphrase Voltaire's philosophy.

ultimately be the winner and another the loser. Without trust, lots of energy is wasted on suspicions, unproductive internal competition, etc.

Trust occurs when there are mutual interests. And since mutual interests rarely occur in the short term, there must be faith that they will occur over time. Thus the common expression "life is give and take": We give now, trusting that the receiving will happen later on.

How can we manifest trust on a global level? We need to eradicate the remnants of a colonialist attitude, where the dominant entity benefits at the expense of the dominated entity. There must be give and take. We must start thinking at this higher level, looking at common rather than individual interests.

When we broaden our definition of what constitutes self-interest to include the interests of the globe as a whole, the problems immediately rise to the surface, numerous but also easy to see: The air pollution of China is threatening the air quality of California. The destruction of the tropical forests of Brazil is threatening air quality worldwide. In short, we are interdependent; if each country continues to act as if its individual interests supersede all others', these problems will never be resolved. The best we will do is move our problems around the globe from country to country like a game of musical chairs. Inevitably, they will be back, as crises, to haunt us. All of us.

> *We are interdependent; if each country continues to act as if its individual interests supersede all the others', these problems will never be resolved.*

If we are interdependent, we must also be collaborative. What we have now is a disaster: non-collaborative interdependence. This state of affairs is doomed to failure.

As a civilization, are we going to succeed or fail?

PREDICTING SUCCESS

For decades, social scientists have been trying to determine the most important factor in economic success (defined unidimensionally as economic growth): Is it technology? A free market? The availability of natural resources? Market size? High levels of investment? Job creation? Competition? Social protections?

I have dedicated my life to studying this question, and I have found out that success, no matter how it is defined, is a function of one variable, which is a function of four variables, which in turn are caused by four other variables, etc. At the bottom of this pyramid of variables, there might be a million factors.[9]

But what is the single variable at the top of the pyramid? Culture. The biggest asset any system can have—whether it is a person, a family, a business organization, or a country—is a culture that promotes mutual trust and respect.

It is this factor that will dictate the amount of energy available for the system to integrate itself with the environment in which it operates, which is the condition for success of any system, any way it is measured.

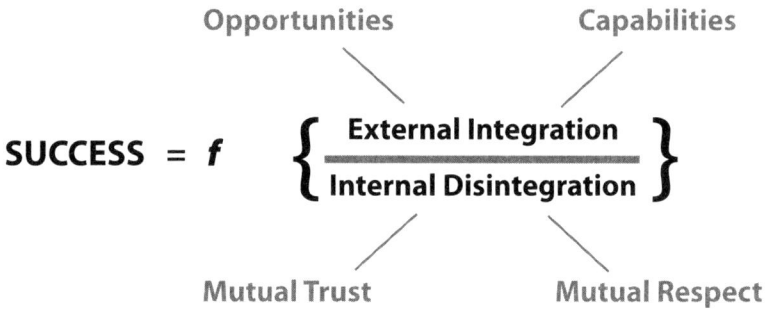

$$\text{SUCCESS} = f \left\{ \frac{\text{External Integration}}{\text{Internal Disintegration}} \right\}$$

Opportunities   Capabilities

Mutual Trust   Mutual Respect

External integration is a function of how well an organization meets the demands of the environment in which it operates. It is a function of how well the system matches its changing capabilities to the changing needs of the environment it serves. For an individual, it can be measured by how much energy is spent to achieve a successful career. In the business world, it is measured by the energy spent to reach a desirable market share. For a country, it is how much energy must be devoted to implementing a successful industrial or economic policy, to allow that country to fit well into the global economy.

Internal disintegration is measured by how much energy is wasted unpro-

[9] For more information on the elements of success, see my book *Mastering Change: The Power of Mutual Trust and Respect in Personal Life, Family, Business, and Society* (Santa Barbara: Adizes Institute Publications, 1993).

ductively on internal suspicions, politics, backbiting, miscommunication, etc.

When a system is well integrated internally, it operates smoothly, accomplishing its tasks without wasting precious energy on destructive internal conflicts.

The more mutual trust and respect, the less internal disintegration there will be.

Why is this significant?

Well, we know from physics that energy is fixed at any point in time, which means any energy spent on internal disintegration is not available for external integration.

When mutual trust and respect are strong, internal disintegration is low and more energy is available for external integration. When mutual trust and respect are low, internal disintegration is high: Much energy is wasted on internal conflicts, and since energy is fixed, little is left for external integration.

What I have discovered is that this fixed energy is allocated in a predictable order: First, it is used to handle internal disintegration; only the surplus, if any, is dedicated to external integration.

For example, if an individual is sick, he has no energy left to make changes that are necessary to adapt to a changing environment. And by "sick," I do not necessarily mean physically sick. Let's assume this person has no self-respect or self-trust. His energy will be spent wondering what people think of him, and doubting every decision he makes. He will be overloaded with internal conflicts that do not leave sufficient energy to deal with his external problems.

The same is true for a company. If there are destructive, "political" conflicts inside a company with no mutual trust and respect, lots of energy is wasted on internal frictions—to the point that when a customer arrives, we might have to say: "Please come back tomorrow; I have spent all my time in meetings trying to protect my turf, and I am exhausted."

The same is true for a country. Notice which countries are economically successful; they are not necessarily those with major natural resources or technology. Rather, they are the ones that have and cultivate a culture of mutual trust and respect. Switzerland and Japan, for instance. And the United States. What characterizes the United States is its acceptance of diversity and the prohibition, by law, of discrimination by religion, race, or gender. That is why, all over the world, America is known as the country where "the sky's the limit"—where people have an unlimited potential for success.

In contrast, what happens to a country that has enormous natural resources, but internal lack of mutual trust and respect? Take South Africa or Angola, for instance. We all know the answer to that.

What makes a system successful is not what it has, but what it is. It is its culture.

THE CONDITIONS FOR CONSTRUCTIVE CONFLICT

Now the question is: how to build mutual trust and respect.

We cannot expect to simply have it and build on it. As a matter of fact, the more frequent and significant the changes, the more vulnerable mutual trust and respect become: More problems to be solved mean more potentially destructive conflicts. Repetitive stress, over time, can dissipate mutual trust and respect, unless we develop the means to nurture our diversity and tolerate our differences.

How can that be done?

I have found that there are four elements that together can transform a system's culture into one in which there is constructive conflict based on mutual trust and respect. Those factors are:

- common vision and values;
- a functional structure (global governance);
- the right decision-making process; and
- people with the right attitude.

Let's discuss what these four elements mean on a global scale.

COMMON VISION AND VALUES

In order for our civilization to avoid accelerating toward destructive conflict, we need a shared global vision of a society different from the one we live in today. In this vision, interdependencies are recognized for the benefit of all rather than for a few. The fact that we have different cultures is not seen as a threat but as an asset. Rights and protections are accorded not only to people but also to animals and to the physical environment we live in— our air, water, and land. We cannot continue destroying other elements to maximize our own benefits. I repeat: We cannot be interdependent without becoming collaborative.

President Barack Obama has made it a mantra in many of his speeches that we need a global solution for global problems, based on "mutual respect and mutual interests." (Note that mutual interests are what *cause* mutual trust, so we are talking about the same thing using different words.)

But we all know that good intentions are not enough. Beyond a new global vision based on mutual trust and respect, we need a structure to deliver this new philosophy.

A FUNCTIONAL STRUCTURE (GLOBAL GOVERNANCE)

We need to see the emergence of an umbrella organization that is structured to represent the interests of the globe as a whole, instead of as an aggregation of individual countries' interests like the UN.

Who will comprise this decision-making body? A holistic problem requires a holistic solution, and that calls for gathering together a group of powerful people representing complementary disciplines that include all of the coalesced authority, power, and influence (CAPI) necessary to implement a solution.[10] That also means that institutions with the capability to undermine the decision must be included—because in my experience, the people who row the boat don't rock the boat.

Why do we need a group that has CAPI? Because approaching decisions the way civilization has done up to now is no longer effective. We have to create an institution with decision-making powers where individual or national interests, together with representatives of non-political elements of society, can combine to mold cohesive policies that serve everyone. With all the levers of power included, the group would have the power and ability to make change.

In addition to politicians, this new global institution should include representatives of the major multinational companies; the leading artists,

---

[10] For more information on CAPI (coalesced authority, power, and influence), see *Mastering Change*, chapter 7.

academics, and scientists; religious leaders; and the magnates of the global media.

We must also include the technologists and intelligentsia—those who have specific knowledge of how to do what needs to be done. These are not necessarily the people who are responsible for making or implementing decisions; in fact, I have often found that when there is disintegration, those who have the authority to say "yes" and "no" often lack the power to implement their decisions—nor do they necessarily have the knowledge to make good decisions. Conversely, those who have the information and knowledge lack the power or the authority. Worst of all, those who have the power to undermine decisions often have little or no knowledge concerning those decisions. They are merely destructive forces, without the expertise or authority to build anything.

THE RIGHT DECISION-MAKING PROCESSES

We still think of problem-solving as a sequence—that economic change will bring social change, which will bring political change; or that political change will bring economic change, which will bring social change. … But the environment is changing far too fast to accommodate this kind of linear development of solutions. What is needed is a systemic approach: all of the components discussed together and at the same time.

THE RIGHT ATTITUDE

What do I mean by the "right" attitude? We need people who do not fear conflict and who know how to convert it into a constructive force. They must be people who command and grant trust and respect to others who are different in style and interests.

That means a major change in our system of education. At present, we teach competition rather than collaboration—in sports, but also in business and even in science.

There is a need to value, to experience, and to teach collaboration and mutual trust and respect. It should be a major component of our education system globally.

ZERO TOLERANCE FOR TYRANNY

So, our civilization is faced with this stark choice: We can move along a path toward destruction—a nuclear disaster unprecedented in the history of mankind, or a long, continuous struggle with terrorism—or we can choose to adopt a new global philosophy: a culture of mutual trust and respect that converts the inevitable conflicts, created by inevitable change, into a constructive force.

Stopping change is not a reasonable solution. Forbidding diversity is a disaster in the short run and does not work in the long run. There is only one good option: We have to commit ourselves to developing a global vision, structure, decision-making process, and attitude that can nourish diversity and ensure constructive conflict.

If diversity is imperative, does that mean we must also tolerate political parties or religious groups that reject diversity? Shouldn't being "pro-diversity" mean tolerance of those who are against diversity?

No.

The late Harvard professor Samuel Huntington, in his famed 1993 *Foreign Affairs* article "The Clash of Civilizations?"[11] and later in his book *The Clash of Civilizations and the Remaking of World Order*,[12] argued that since the fall of Communism, the most serious international conflicts have not been between economic classes or military powers, or even between nations, but between "cultures," roughly grouped and allied by their shared religion, history, language, and tradition.

In order to survive, Huntington argued, the West must reaffirm, strengthen, and protect Western culture. How? It should forge strong alliances with similar liberal Western nations. In particular, it must not weaken itself in the name of diversity by integrating alien and incompatible customs into its way of life.

My position is similar: We cannot allow anti-diversity theories, regimes, or cultures to flourish in our midst ("live and let live") and endanger our own system of values and our vision of a society based on mutual trust and

---

[11] Samuel P. Huntington, "The Clash of Civilizations?" *Foreign Affairs*, Summer 1993, pp. 22-49.

[12] Samuel P. Huntington, *The Clash of Civilizations and the Remaking of World Order* (New York: Simon & Schuster, 1996).

respect. We should not nurture that which will cause destructive conflict and possibly even destroy us.

I believe democratic systems are too tolerant of non-democratic forces. Among political scientists there is continual debate about whether democracies should allow non-democratic parties to exist. In an environment in which the rate of change was not so intense, I would feel differently; freedom of speech would take precedence. But when the rate of change is acute, and the ambiguity and uncertainty and pain from that acuteness is overwhelming, the danger is that simple-minded people who don't understand the complexity of a problem will try to find a simple solution, and that is almost always an extreme solution.

Totalitarianism offers clarity in black and white. It's simple and clear, unlike the ambiguity that democracies offer. That is why totalitarianism, diversity-averse entities, and fatalistic cults have a significant advantage during periods of great change. That's why, as the rate of change increases, so does the cacophony of religious revivals and vocal minorities, whether they are fanatical Muslims, Jews, or Christians. It is another manifestation of the rate of change.

But the more these movements gain, the more they endanger diversity.

In this volatile environment, I believe that no one should be permitted to undermine the system or the democratic vision, or to foment racial unrest. All subversive, exclusive, or excluding fanatical entities should be banned, and educational systems should be put in place that are geared toward inclusion, diversity, and tolerance.

Globally, we can't ban or outlaw governments that are reactionary, intolerant, and anti-diverse. But we do not have to work with them, either. Solutions require constructive conflict, which requires mutual trust and respect—which cannot happen, by definition, with groups that do not share the same vision and values, groups that are planning the destruction of other groups.

Instead, we need to freeze out these anti-diversity regimes and insulate ourselves against their destructive culture. Eventually, isolated from the free world and without the tools to harness conflict constructively, they will collapse by themselves, like the Soviet Union and Yugoslavia.

Globally, our goals—what we are looking for and what we should do about it—will evolve and clarify over time, as each nation adapts itself to rapid and intense change and brings its perspective to the international table.

I firmly believe that the road to a solution still exists. It may not be the road we are used to traveling, and it may not have the landmarks we're used to seeing, but it is there, waiting to be discovered.

Time grows short, however.

TAKING RESPONSIBILITY[1]

I was on a consulting assignment in Berlin on November 9, 2008, and across from my hotel, I noticed a building with Hebrew letters. In front of the building there were hundreds of floral arrangements placed along the fence.

"What is going on?" I asked a policeman standing guard at the gate.

"It is Kristallnacht, and this is the Jewish center," he told me.

Kristallnacht ("Crystal Night") was the name given to the night of November 9, 1938, in Germany, when a state-sponsored anti-Semitic riot resulted in the destruction of thousands of Jewish establishments. The "demonstrators" broke all the windows of Jewish stores and frightened people away from doing business with Jews. It is remembered as the beginning of official Nazi government persecution of the Jews.

Each year on the anniversary of that infamous day, many German organizations put flowers in front of the Jewish center.

On that day, I also observed a solemn procession of approximately a thousand people walking to and from the Brandenburg Gate. These could not have been Jewish people; there are not very many left in Germany. These Germans were demonstrating to call attention to the shame of Kristallnacht and ensure that what followed will "never again" be allowed to occur.

Germany's memorial to the victims of the Holocaust, a stark cemetery-like line of cement blocks of different heights, is located in the middle of Berlin, next to the world-famous Brandenburg Gate, which is visited by millions every year. Because of that proximity, it is impossible to miss the memorial. It is there for all to see and visit.

At the entrance to the memorial is a museum of the Holocaust, which documents, in words and pictures, the atrocities committed by the Nazis.

To me, this museum is much more moving than *Yad Vashem*,

---

[1] Adizes Insights, March 2009.

the Holocaust museum in Jerusalem, or the one in Washington, D.C. In addition, the atrocities are better documented and displayed. I even found the names of my grandparents on the list of those deported to Treblinka, and a picture of the concentration camp I was in.

FOLLOWING GERMANY'S EXAMPLE

Germany's Holocaust museum made me wonder about other countries that have perpetrated crimes against humanity. Do other nations admit their wrongdoings and memorialize them? I cannot think of any other country that washes its dirty laundry in public like this. Is there a memorial in Russia to the millions of Ukrainian *kulaks* murdered by the Bolsheviks? Is there a memorial in Turkey to the Armenians slaughtered in 1915; or in Japan, to the Chinese killed by the Japanese army during World War II; or in Serbia, to the atrocities committed in Bosnia?

We memorialize *our own* pain; but what about the pain we inflict on others?

Pursuing this train of thought, it occurred to me: There will be no peace in the Middle East (nor in any marriage, for that matter) till each of us can feel the other's pain.

> There will be no peace in the Middle East (nor in any marriage, for that matter) till each of us can feel the other's pain.

The Germans are giving us an example that the whole world should follow.

I suggest that one day should be chosen each year, not just as a memorial for the Jewish Holocaust: It should be a day of forgiveness, when every country should ask forgiveness from those it has harmed. This is the day the Turks will march to acknowledge the horrors committed against the Armenians. And the Armenians will march to acknowledge the pain inflicted on the Turks. Japan will acknowledge its crimes against the Chinese, and the Americans against the Native Americans. And people from all walks of life, from the grass roots—women, men, old, and young—should demonstrate to support the proposition "Never again," like the Germans do.

No blaming of the other should be permitted. Let us stop looking for who is at fault. Let us just acknowledge the pain we inflict on each other. That is all we need to do—one day annually. We can do the blaming the rest of the year.

THE ROLE
OF MANAGEMENT EDUCATION
IN DEVELOPING ECONOMIES[1]

CEEMAN President Professor Purg, deans, professors, ladies and gentlemen:

The theme of my presentation is globalization and its impact on management education.

What qualifications do I have to lecture on this subject? I have done no scientific survey whatsoever, but I *have* lectured to thousands of top executives in fifty-two countries and consulted in half of those countries over a period of forty years.

In addition, as my books, over time, were translated into twenty-six languages, I learned that very competent translators had difficulties translating my theories of management, because there are no words in those languages for the theories I discuss. These experiences have given me insights into the state of management education and practices globally. I would like to share those insights with you today.

It is no secret that Western—mainly American—theories and practices of management are spreading around the world like wildfire. American titans of industry are putting in writing their practice of management, as Lee Iacocca and Jack Welch have recently done, and their books are being translated and worshiped like prayer books. Western business schools, again mainly American, are opening branches all over the world, teaching American management theories and practices as well as the functional disciplines of marketing, finance, supply-chain management, etc.

I suggest, however, that what is being spread around the world is not a

---

[1] Keynote presentation to the Central and East European Management Development Association (CEEMAN), presented at Sabanci University, Istanbul, Turkey, September 27, 2007.

benign, value-free, logical, systemic process. I suggest to you that what is being spread *with* the theory and practice of management is a value-*loaded* political philosophy.

It came as a surprise to me that the word "management" has no translation in any other language—except Hebrew, I believe. Everyone uses the English word—even the French, who have made an ideology out of using only French words.

In Spanish, they have the words *administración* and *dirección,* but again, no word for "management." In fact, in Spanish, the word *manejar* (to manage) refers to the handling of horses or cars only.

Actually, the metaphor of handling cars or horses is not far-fetched.

Having searched many English dictionaries for synonyms for the concept "to manage," I have found that the common denominator of all of the synonyms is their assumption that management, as a process, is a one-way flow of energy: *I*, the manager, the executive, the leader (different words with the same elitist connotation: "I am management; you are not"), decide what the organization should do, and then *I* order the organization to execute those wishes. I am managing well if *I* choose well where to go, and if the car or the horse—those I manage—execute *my* plans.

My content analysis of management books, theory, and trade reinforced this observation. Here are some of the synonyms I found in those books: "to govern," "to control," "to handle," "to manipulate," "to plan for," "to dominate," "to decide for." Put in this context, the concept "to motivate" is synonymous with "to manipulate": *I* know what *I* want *you* to do. The only question is: How do I *motivate* you—i.e., how do *I* make *you* want to do what *I* want you to do?

> American schools of management are spreading non-democratic processes of management around the world.

So how can we define the concept of "leadership" in organizations? Here is what Dwight D. Eisenhower had to say about it: "Leadership is the art of getting someone else to do something that *you* want done, because *he* wants to do it." (The italics are mine.) Here is what Japanese executive Konosuke Matsushita says: "The essence of management is getting the ideas out of the heads of the bosses—and into the hands of labor."

Do you notice that this process is a one-way flow of energy—i.e., non-democratic? *Those who are governed have no say about how they will be governed and who will govern them.*

Listen to the words "supervisor" and "subordinate." "Supervisor" originates from the words "*superior* vision," and "*subordinate*" contains the prefix "*sub,*" meaning "beneath." Management is not only a process. It defines a class structure, too. Did you realize that the system is elitist?

Granted, with the advent of the "new economy," the Internet, and high tech, there is pressure to depart from this elitist, non-democratic paradigm of management. "Knowledgeable workers" are the source of knowledge and initiative. They are well educated and have aspirations for self-actualization, for self-expression. The latest theories of management take this into account and prescribe less elitism and more participation. There are no "workers" anymore—only "associates." But except for very few professional organizations such as consultants' organizations, the essence, or the paradigm, of *non-democratic elitism* has not changed. Those who are managed have no say in who manages them or how.

Isn't it ironic that American schools of management are spreading these non-democratic processes of management around the world, while at the same time thousands of American soldiers are dying in Iraq and Afghanistan trying to spread democracy?

This elitist, non-democratic paradigm of management emerged because the founding fathers of management theory derived their insights about the process from their own experiences with hierarchically structured, non-democratically managed industrial or military organizations. It is true that the human relations school of management introduced by Elton Mayo initiated concern for the human element, and from that emerged the field of behavioral science. But it did not change the paradigm. None of the subsequent gurus, theory leaders, and practicing geniuses changed the paradigm, either. It is still essentially a one-directional flow of energy: *I* am management and *you* are hereby being managed. You have no institutional way to choose whether I will be your leader or not, nor do you have the right to influence how I exercise my authority over you. You can't even replace me—but I can replace you.

In other words, the system is, at best, benign authoritarianism. This whole framework, I suggest, resembles parent-child relations, and this might explain why management theory seemed familiar rather than odd as it was developed and taught, and as it is currently being practiced.

EXPORTING NON-DEMOCRATIC PROCESSES

What are the repercussions of globalizing this paradigm?

I suggest to you that practicing this paradigm in a country in transition, or in a developing country that was once a colony, could undermine the country's emerging political democratic process. To start, people in these emerging economies do not feel they are part of the organization they work for, because the organization was once owned either by the government or by foreigners. The workers had no voice. Why would they now, all at once, believe that they can affect the macro political environment, when in the past and still, at present, they are muted, impotent, and deprived of influence and a vote about their own immediate environment, where they spend most of their waking hours?

An elitist, non-democratic management system only reinforces their sense of alienation.

Granted, there is evidence that common people rise to demand democracy and are ready to die for it, but this tends to occur only after extreme, prolonged oppression. A single violent reaction to dictatorship is not an adequate substitute for sustainable, institutionalized participation in political processes, which will nurture a democratizing cultural transformation.

Management, as taught and practiced, does not nourish this transformation. On the contrary, and as discussed so far, it undermines it. Moreover, elitist management promotes class distinctions and polarization. It promotes a rewards system in which executives might be paid one hundred times the salary of a worker.

In the United States, where there is a significant and politically involved middle class, this practice might have only a marginal political impact. In emerging economies, however, it establishes a system in which those who have, have lots, and see themselves as politically powerful; whereas those who have little, if any, perceive themselves as marginalized and impotent, without the power to promote their own interests democratically.

And the repercussions? Widespread depression and apathy of the masses, who are doomed to pain and hopelessness. Violence and disruption are the only vehicles available to create change or manifest some power.

Of course, current management practice has characteristics beyond elitism and non-democratic processes.

Management theory and practice, especially in the United States, is based on the "hidden hand" theory of Adam Smith, which states that competition—adversarial relations, in a free market—will in time produce the optimal allocation of resources. This framework does not factor in the cost of human emotions. It is pure materialistic economics, consistent with Thomas Hobbes' philosophy that "Man is a wolf to other men." Adversity is not only tolerated but seen as legitimate; the system takes it for granted that management and workers will be at odds with each other.

A rich country like the United States can afford disruptions such as strikes, but for a budding economy, an adversarial culture that might temporarily paralyze the country with a nationwide strike can be prohibitive.

TRADITION OF INDIVIDUALISM

But developing countries and countries in transition are not only importing elitism, adversarial relations, and a non-democratic philosophy and practice. There is more to it. Western theory and practice of management are based on the American culture of individualism: The individual entrepreneur takes the risk of starting a company to fulfill his dream. Since he is aware that he is taking these risks as an individual, he also has the authority, as an individual, to make decisions. Although public companies can emerge from those start-ups, in which ownership is separated from management and boards of directors make decisions as a group, the paradigm of individualism has not changed. Now it's the CEO, elected by the board and reporting to the board, who still has an individual responsibility to produce results or else be replaced.

This individual accountability permeates all the way down to the last person in a managerial position. Participation in decision-making is not a cornerstone of American culture. In this culture, more than any other (although the Chinese are catching up rapidly), time is money. And since participative management takes time, it is perceived, at best, as a necessary evil.

What is wrong with the tradition of individualism?

Individualism fosters loneliness, and not only at the top. It permeates, by and large, all the managerial ranks. In a rapidly changing environment, which by definition means rapidly emerging new problems that need to be dealt with, loneliness means continuous and relentless stress.

And it isn't only executives who suffer from stress. Workers suffer too, from the lack of genuine attention to their needs. New, freshly trained MBA managers have very limited, if any, experience of what it means to sweat it on the line. If they interned anywhere before becoming managers, it was in serving management, not in doing the actual work.

In developed countries, organizations are large and physically scattered. Workers are merely a name and a number, and business school-trained managers, who have never worked on the line, rarely have empathy for those they manage. They are more sensitive to the financial variations, which they endlessly labored on at school. If they do have some sensitivity to workers, I have observed that it is a learned trait and is thus cerebral; it does not come genuinely from the heart and soul.

The result of all this is a culture comprising a mad dash for the dollar; a pressured environment to meet ever-rising goals; adversarial relations both in the market and in the workplace; loneliness at the top as well as throughout managerial ranks; and a lack of genuine sensitivity to those managed. And what I have just described does not end at the workplace. It migrates to the social and personal environment as well.

> *Individualism fosters loneliness, and not only at the top. It permeates, by and large, all the managerial ranks.*

So what is being exported is more than the new word "management." What developing countries are importing is a culture and political process that impacts families, friendships, and the social fabric of society—and is often called "Americanization."

QUALITY-OF-LIFE ISSUES

Although in the United States the standard of living is higher than in developing countries, I have observed that the quality of life is lower. People do not have the time to enjoy each other's company, to celebrate each other. Starbucks is a pale substitute for the European coffee shop, where socializing is considered a goal in itself, and people socialize for hours. As a result, we Americans do not affiliate enough, and this basic need is inadequately fulfilled. In spite of having three cars in the garage and more than one chicken in the pot, people are lonely.

Depression is the most prevalent mental disease of developed countries. In emerging countries, on the other hand, if they are not at war, people may be poor but you often see genuine smiles and genuine interest and joy at being with each other. I hear much more laughter and many more sing-alongs.

Thus, our management education promotes a culture that increases economic bounty at the expense of emotional and social fulfillment, and does not promote democracy.

There is another problem with management education. It is based on economic and political conditions that are prevalent in developed economies (primarily in the West), but significantly different from the emerging countries to which we export that education.

One day I was lecturing to top management in New Delhi, India. The subject was marketing: how to gain competitive advantage in the marketplace. During the break, an executive came over to explain something: "Marketing strategy is important for you Americans," he said, "but is not as critical for us here. For us, knowing how the government operates is much more critical than knowing the market. Government and its bureaucracy can be the biggest and best barrier to competition. Knowing how to work with a bureaucracy gives us a competitive advantage. It is much more critical than competitive posturing in the marketplace."

Do management schools in emerging economies teach anything about government relations, about networking, about the ethical issues of lobbying government, about how to work with and around a bureaucracy?

In emerging economies, capital markets are not very efficient. Market intelligence is not available. Skilled labor is not easily accessible. Since access to information is limited and the court system is ineffective or corrupt, people in these countries will not do business with you until they trust you, or until someone they trust vouches for you. For them, trust is critical for success, while in the West, instead of trust, organizations rely on lawyers and contracts and the court system to guarantee that they get what was agreed upon.

Are we teaching how to create and nurture circles of trust, which are indispensable factors for success in developing countries and those in transition, or do we translate, copy, and take brief junkets to such countries just to teach the same stuff we teach at, say, Harvard? How arrogant can we be?

ONE SIZE DOES NOT FIT ALL

What about decision-making? Different cultures decide differently, and the American custom does not fit all cultures. In the United States, it is usually possible to discuss problems openly, whereas in China, encouraging open discussion of problems can backfire, because the same discussion would be perceived as criticism, perhaps even public humiliation, of top management.

Here is another difference: In Italy or Greece, if there is disagreement during decision-making meetings, it will be expressed right away. People will not be silent. In those two countries, if people are silent you can assume that they agree with what is being said.

But in Germany and Scandinavia, silence does not mean agreement at all. Just the opposite: If there is silence, that means there is general disagreement, because people in those countries are not accustomed to expressing disagreement in open discussion. As multinational corporations evolve, they have more and more difficulty integrating the different cultures and managerial practices they encounter. The "one size fits all" American system is not the answer.

Here is another point about culture: In totalitarian regimes, everything is prohibited unless specifically permitted. In market economies and democracies, everything is permitted unless specifically forbidden.

In countries in transition, those people who made the transition early made a lot of money and emerged as the new entrepreneurial elite. Those who could not, found themselves economically trapped.

Are business schools in countries in transition helping their students to make these major cultural and psychological adjustments, or do they straightforwardly teach Western theories and practices, assuming their students are already adjusted?

So far I have been focusing on management as an integrative process, not as a functional discipline. But the same analysis applies to functional management. Granted, finance is finance, but it's crucial to pay attention to local financial markets and needs and teach micro-banking, for instance, rather than derivative financial vehicles. And I wonder how much value we really add by teaching sophisticated supply-chain management processes and mathematical models of inventory control in countries where collusion and corruption dominate the supply chain. Instead of teaching Markoff chains, we should first and above all delegitimize collusion, showing students how corruption destroys a system and teaching them how to eradicate it.

But do we know how to do that? Are we teaching what people *need* to know, or just what *we* know?

CULTURAL COLONIALISM

What is happening, I suggest, is a form of cultural colonialism, and management schools are among its major "carriers" (another being the media). I do not believe it is planned or even intentional. Most people are simply unaware of the cultural, political, and social dimensions hidden in Western management training.

Why are Western—again, mainly American—theories and practices of management so welcome worldwide? Why is American management theory spreading exponentially?

Despite all the criticism and resistance to America, I have observed that the world is in awe of American success. The word "America" evokes images of Cadillacs and villas with swimming pools; easily available sex; freedom to speak out; and freedom to advance without being limited by age, color, gender, or ethnic affiliation. America is synonymous with freedom and material abundance, and "America" and "California" are emotionally loaded words.

Everyone criticizes America, but given the choice they would love to have an American degree, an American passport, and for sure an American standard of living. I believe that, enchanted with "America," the world believes that America's success must have something to do with how its companies are managed.

But let me tell you something: Some American companies are so badly managed, even though their leaders have MBAs from leading universities— *so* badly managed that anywhere else in the world they would go bankrupt;

they would simply not be able to withstand the difficulties and challenges. I have had personal experience with some of these companies. They stay in business because America is an enormously big market that can "forgive" mistakes for a while; its systems—capital, transportation, telephones—work better than in the rest of the world. So these managers succeed in spite of themselves. As they say in the Silicon Valley, "In a typhoon, even turkeys fly."

In developing countries or those in transition, by contrast, the electricity and the phone service stop from time to time. Corruption, starting with the court system, is widespread. Bureaucracy rules. Universal education is still a dream. Inflation can be rampant. The government can freeze corporate cash assets in the banks, as they did in Brazil. Unpredictable changes in import quotas and widely fluctuating exchange rates are like shock treatments that cause prolonged "managerial dizziness."

Managing in that environment requires ingenuity, intelligence, creativity, courage, resoluteness, and much more original thinking and resilience than what is required in an established market like the United States.

I suggest that Western management education does not provide the real-life know-how that the graduates in emerging countries need in order to succeed. I suggest that America's greatest success is not its management system but its market economy and its democratic system, which allow and nurture constructive diversity.

The managerial practices we teach and export neither nurture democracy nor support constructive diversity of styles and interests. On the contrary, what we teach, practice, and spread around the world *undermines* democracy, by teaching benevolent dictatorship.

A Paradigm Shift

A new paradigm of management theory is needed: a *universal* theory that is culture-free, industry-neutral, and non-elitist; that nurtures democratic processes and social relations, and that produces superior economic results.

I am proud to report to you that I have been developing a new paradigm theory over the last thirty or forty years, and I have tested it in more than fifty-two countries, in both industrial and non-industrial environments, such as performing arts organizations, governments, health delivery systems, and educational institutions. Thousands of people all over the world have been trained and are practicing it, and several hundred are certified to teach it. This methodology is transferable and produces predictable, superior economic results. It is covered in my books, videos, and audio recordings, as well as in thousands of pages of manuals,[2] and it has been recognized by several educational institutions, which have awarded me honorary doctorates.

Let me give you some insight as to what it is. Necessarily, I will have to be brief.

Let me start with a definition of "management," a definition that is free of cultural bias or limitations of size, and even of goals. It is applicable to both for-profit and not-for-profit organizations. Furthermore, it is also non-specific to any particular industry.

What is management? It is a process people practice to make the organization effective and efficient in the short and in the long run. If the entity being managed is not effective or efficient—now or in the future—then it is not being managed well. (Some languages have no literal translation for either word: Russian has no word for "efficiency"; in Hebrew, there is no word for "effectiveness.")

Now please note that whoever causes the organization to be effective or efficient now and in the future takes part in management. Management is a function, not an elite class distinction. For instance, workers on the line, salesmen, and others, often know what the clients want better than management does. Their involvement and commitment are indispensable for making the organization effective. They are the ones who are on the front line satisfying the clients' needs—which is the reason the organization exists.

> Each country should develop specific, indigenous training practices that use its strengths to overcome the weaknesses in its culture.

I have discovered that there are four roles of management that, if performed well, will make the organization effective and efficient, now and in the future.

These roles are:

(P), for (P)roducing the results for which the organization exists, which by definition means that the organization is *effective in the short run.*

---

[2] See the Adizes website, www.adizes.com, for a list of my books, videos, and articles, as well as testimonials and references.

To be *efficient in the short run*, the organization must be organized, systematized, and programmed, so that no energy is wasted reinventing the wheel. That is the role of (A)dministration, the (A) role.

To be *effective in the long run*, the organization has to be proactive. That means that it needs to predict the future needs of its present and future clients, and then it needs to prepare now to serve those needs in that uncertain future. That entails risk-taking, because no one knows for sure what the future holds. To be proactive requires the (E) role, (E)ntrepreneuring. (Here again it is interesting that some languages—Swedish, for instance—do not have a word that means "entrepreneuring"; and in other cultures, the word exists but has negative connotations. Under Communism, "entrepreneurship" was tantamount to speculation and the sabotaging of the state, and was a punishable offense.)

Finally, to be *efficient in the long run*, the organization should not rely on any single individual for its survival. The organization must be integrated—the (I) role. The (I)ntegrator pays attention to the human element: how people work together and why.

No Perfect Manager

What I have also discovered is that no individual manager, executive, leader, or parent can perform all four roles at the same time and excel in them all. In other words, the "ideal" executive that organizations need to be successful, in the short and in the long run, does not and cannot exist.

My discovery is that (what a surprise!) no one is perfect. We are *all* mismanagers. Some more, some less. We are all human, with strengths and weaknesses. The managerial process is far too complicated for any single individual to excel in it all.

The present paradigm of management education is based on the mistaken assumption that the ideal manager can be developed or trained; that an individual, all by himself, can manage well. Billions of dollars are being spent in trying to produce hens' teeth. We should stop training individuals in a vacuum and start training them as members of a complementary team.

Please note that I am not referring to "collaborative leadership," which is a newly emerging fad. Collaborative leadership takes the position that you do not know it all, so you need to work with people who know what you don't know. But I am not talking about *knowing*. I am talking about *being*. We need different personal styles working together.

Why? Because the person who excels in the entrepreneurial role is a risk-taker. He moves fast and thinks in generalities. This role is necessary for keeping the organization innovative and flexible, but it can also destroy an organization and take it into bankruptcy. How? Entrepreneurs are usually not detail-oriented, and as we know, the Devil is often in the details. What an entrepreneur needs is a cool-headed, slow-thinking, complementary co-leader who is risk-averse. Together they will make much better decisions than either of them could make alone.

And they might even need a third person, a producer, who is action-oriented, who wants to see results, movement—not just the excitement of creating something new and analyzing the risks involved.

And if all three team members lack sensitivity to people, they will need a fourth person—an integrator—who will bring that sensitivity to bear on the decisions being made.

Successful management is not and cannot be performed by an individual. It is a team process. Like parenting. In our management schools, we need to teach that in order to succeed, managers need to complement themselves. They need people whose style is different from theirs. They, as individuals, cannot excel at managing, regardless of how well they succeeded in solving cases at school.

Each member of the team is as important as another. True, one is the leader, *primus inter pares*, but without the others, her decisions will eventually lead the organization to failure, because those decisions are necessarily biased by style. It is the joint judgment of different and complementary styles that creates the necessary balance for making the organization effective and efficient in the present and in the future.

Worker Participation

Furthermore, organizations, to succeed, need the workers' cooperation. In this tested and practiced methodology, workers should sit on the board and on lower management committees, thus sharing the responsibility for leading the company. We need to work together, consider each other's interests, and deal with them proactively, rather than reactively when there is already a crisis. When workers share the interests of the owners and thus cooperate, the company will make successful changes faster. That is critical for a company operating in a changing environment. Workers should be part of the managerial *process* even though they are not considered part of the managerial *ranks*. In this case, those in the managerial role are different, but please note: They are not special.

Our future leaders have to recognize that by definition, a complementary team composed of different styles and different interests will be loaded with conflicts. Conflicts are to be expected and can be constructive rather than destructive when there is a culture of mutual trust and respect: trust that common interests do exist in the long run, although in the short run there might be none; and the respect to hear and learn from people who, because of their different styles, disagree with us.

Good managers know their style limitations, work well with others who are different from them, and are not afraid of conflict. They surround themselves with people they trust and are open to hearing what those people disagree about. They create a climate of mutual trust and respect.

We need to teach countries in transition how to build and nurture such a culture. For that, a common vision and common values are needed, as well as an organizational architecture that nurtures diversity of styles. Those learning to become managers need to learn how to lead decision-making sessions in which people with different styles have to jointly make a decision. They must also learn whom to hire to design a complementary team with the correct components.

They should know how to convert conflict from a destructive force to a constructive one, to control their own egos, and to create teamwork. In other words, what makes a good manager is not what he *knows* but what he *is*: a person who commands and grants trust, respect, and humility. That should be common management training in all countries.

INDIGENOUS TRAINING

In addition to the principles above, each country should develop specific, indigenous training practices that use its strengths to overcome the weaknesses in its culture. In Israel, I suggested they teach more administration:

systems, order, procedures, rules, discipline—skills that entrepreneurs often lack.

To the Japanese, on the other hand, I proposed that they learn individual entrepreneurship. They need to revamp their whole educational system, which is based on learning to know, and replace it with knowing how to learn. They need to develop individual creativity and learn to tolerate dissension.

What about the Balkans and the Middle East? We know that one characteristic of those cultures is paranoia. It would be amusing, if it weren't so sad, to watch their executives explain a problem to you: There is always collusion somewhere. There is always a villain rather than a systemic cause. In the Balkans and the Middle East, it is critical to develop training that nurtures mutual trust and respect.

Management education of leaders in different countries should not simply be copied from a culture that does not resemble their own. It has to fit the needs of the country in which they operate, and if it is a multinational company, a universal theory of management is needed: how to work in multicultural teams, not *in spite of* being different, but *because* we are different. Differences enrich us with knowledge we do not have; moreover, they improve our judgment, since deciding alone is naturally biased.

Working with mutual trust and respect, we enrich one another with our differences, experience the essence of democracy, produce better and more sustainable economic results, and work in an environment that enriches us emotionally and socially as well as economically.

I thank you for your attention.

IS TERRORISM
ISRAEL'S PROBLEM?[1]

WHENEVER we do not like something, or something is bothering us, we call it a problem. If it is raining and we get wet, it's a problem. If a spouse is an alcoholic, it's a problem. And the crisis in the Middle East is also a problem.

But calling anything we dislike a problem does not help us solve it. In fact, it actually hampers our ability to solve it, because it does not guide us correctly to mobilize the energies that are necessary for solving it.

Let me suggest that a problem should be defined not only as something we do not like (something undesirable and/or unexpected), but also as something we can *control*—i.e., solve. Can you solve the problem of your spouse's alcoholism? You know you cannot; it is your spouse who must find a solution. And if it is out of your control, if you cannot solve it, then it is not your problem. That is an unfortunate fact.

Another mistake is to define a problem by its cause, by asking, "Why?" *Why* is this person an alcoholic? *Why* are interest rates unpredictable? The assumption is that once you understand the cause of the undesirable fact, then that cause is the problem that needs to be solved.

Instead, the focus should be on *who* can solve the problem. That is the starting point. Without the "anchor" of *who* can do something about the problem, looking for a cause is only an academic exercise. We understand the problem better, but what then?

WHOSE PROBLEM IS TERRORISM?

Now, let us look at the disaster in the Middle East:
The killing and the destruction are undesirable. Those are the facts. But

---

[1] Excerpted from Adizes Insights, August 2006.

whose problem is it?

In the past, Israel could have done better. Much better. And if it had, maybe we would not be in the soup we are in now. But that was then. What about now?

Hezbollah is publicly committed to the destruction of Israel, and they walk their talk. Israel cannot solve this problem, because Israel cannot change Hezbollah's behavior no matter how deep they go into Lebanon and no matter how many guerrillas they kill. There will always be more guerrillas to replace the ones who were killed.

The Lebanese army cannot control Hezbollah, either. Two years ago, the United Nations passed a resolution requiring Lebanon to disarm Hezbollah. What happened? Nothing. They cannot do it!

Syria and Iran might be able to stop Hezbollah. So, is it *their* problem? No, it isn't, because they do not see Hezbollah's actions as undesirable. "What problem?" they would ask.

So, whose problem is it?

Those who can control it.

Who are they?

Disarming Hezbollah would require global pressure, but that will not happen. Look at China, which imports more Iranian oil than any other nation. China could use that leverage to influence Iran. Instead, China actually provides Iran with missiles, in exchange for oil; Iran then passes the missiles on to Hezbollah, which uses them against Israel.

I am coming to the unfortunate conclusion that the problem called "Hezbollah" is not solvable right now, given the present constellation of world powers and their interests. The International Force for Southern Lebanon is a Band-Aid. It will fall apart at the first stressful event. Hezbollah has killed hundreds of U.S. Marines, including 241 Marines in a suicide terror attack in Beirut in 1983.

What will happen if Hezbollah kills hundreds of UN soldiers? Will the international forces go to war against Hezbollah; or will they fold and leave?[2]

---

[2] The United Nations International Force for Southern Lebanon was created in the summer of 2006 by Security Council Resolution 1701. Its purpose was to briefly deploy 15,000 United Nations peacekeepers to help the Lebanese army monitor the cessation of hostilities along the Israel-Lebanon border, to ensure that Hezbollah did not launch further attacks on Israel, and to supervise Israel's withdrawal from Lebanon. In reality, hostilities never ceased. Rockets continue to be fired into Israel from Lebanon, and Hezbollah, sometimes backed by Al-Qaeda, frequently attacks both Israel and the UN

Hezbollah is not alone. Terrorism is a global phenomenon and thus requires a global solution. Such a global solution does not yet exist. It will emerge when all those who are necessary to decide on and implement a solution finally come to see that it is in their interests to get together and do something about it. For that to happen, apparently, the situation has to become much, much worse.

And what will that solution be? Will the international community decide to fight terrorism (including Hezbollah) globally, which is very difficult and risky? Or will it allow Israel to be wiped off the map, as the president of Iran is threatening to do, which could be easier for the world to take? Those who support this solution, or who are prepared to turn a blind eye when it is attempted, must erroneously believe that Israel's disappearance would eliminate terrorism.

> *Terrorism is a global phenomenon and thus requires a global solution. Such a global solution does not yet exist.*

But think: Did Israel cause the emergence of the Taliban, or the terrorism in Chechnya and India?

ISRAEL'S OPTIONS

Since it does not appear that there is a global solution to the global problem, what should Israel do?

Let's go back to the beginning of my argument. First, we must define Israel's problem. What is its problem? Only what it can solve. The fact is that there is no partner on the other side who can make a negotiated solution work. Hamas, like Hezbollah, wants the destruction of Israel, and Hamas is effectively in power in Gaza. Peace-loving Palestinians and Israelis do not have the political power to implement a solution that both parties can agree on.

What can Israel do under those circumstances? Israel has to do whatever it must do to survive—and do it unilaterally if necessary. Like my example above, of the husband or wife married to an alcoholic, Israel has to decide if it wants to stay where it is or leave for some other location.

Except that the prospect of six million Jews relocating anywhere else is

---

soldiers. Every year, the UN passes a resolution extending the force's stay for another year (the current extension will end or be renewed in August 2010). To date, the UN forces have not folded or left—nor have they attempted to solve the problem in any meaningful way.

inconceivable. So Israel has to continue fighting—and fighting hard—for its existence.

Unfortunately, the harder the Israelis fight, the worse the situation gets. It is like some forms of cancer: The more you fight it, the more it spreads. The more the Israelis destroy Hezbollah, the more support Hezbollah will get from the Arab population, and the more militant they will become. The war has no foreseeable ending.

I saw a poster at an Islamic protest that read: "The real Holocaust is coming." I believe they meant every word of it. But this Holocaust, if allowed to happen, will only *start* with Israel. It will not end there, because the Muslim fanatics' war is against *all* infidels.

Israel did not cause the terrors in Afghanistan, in Indonesia, in India, in Madrid, in London, or in Paris. The terrorism against Israel is not an Israeli problem. It is a global problem. And if the world allows Hezbollah and Hamas to win, whose Holocaust will it be then?

Terrorism: An Analysis and a Prediction[1]

To solve a problem, you must first define it. So we must ask: Who and what are terrorists?

Terrorists kill and maim civilians, but so do armies when they fight a war. The casualties at Hiroshima and Nagasaki were not collateral damage; the bombs were dropped knowing there were civilians below. But we do not define those bombings as terrorism.

So what makes terrorists unique? The answer is that terrorists do not communicate with their enemies. They do not negotiate. Their way of dealing with conflict is, "Yield to our demands or experience terror." Terrorists do not compromise. Hamas, for instance, will not agree to anything short of the total disappearance of Israel. And what about al-Qaeda: Does anyone know of a compromise that might convince al-Qaeda to stop its terror attacks?

Dangerous Confusion

Is there a difference between "terrorists" and "liberation fighters"?

Both target civilians, use non-traditional tactics—such as suicide terror attacks—and make non-negotiable demands.

I suggest that the distinction between a "terrorist" and a "liberation fighter" is in the eye of the beholder. For example, during the Algerian uprising against the French in the 1950s, Algeria's French settlers saw the rebellion as terrorism, while Algeria's Muslim population perceived it as a righteous bid for freedom. Another example is the Palestinian suicide terrorists: For those who unequivocally believe in Israel's right to exist, they are terrorists;

---

[1] Adizes Insights, October 2004.

but for those who see Israel as an occupier that needs to be removed from the map, they are freedom fighters.

It is this kind of terminological confusion that gives legitimacy to terrorists, whether they are Chechens, Tamils, or Iraqis, and allows them to hope that their acts will bear the fruits they aim for. And I believe the confusion started in 1974, when Yasser Arafat was allowed to address the General Assembly of the United Nations dressed in his military uniform, with a holster and (by some accounts) a gun on his hip. He received a standing ovation.

In order to design a solution to the problem of terror, we must first agree that it is never legitimate to use force without a willingness to negotiate first and compromise second, no matter how noble the cause—just as our society has taken the position that spousal abuse is unacceptable under any circumstances.

If we start judging terrorist actions by their means rather than their goals, we will erase the distinction between terrorists and freedom fighters. Then, we might be able to see the light at the end of the tunnel.

STEPS TO TAKE

Countries should sign a pact refusing to recognize any state born out of terror. This would automatically deny terrorists/freedom fighters the prize they are fighting for, and thus eliminate the motivation for terrorism.

Chechnya, for example, could not receive world recognition as a sovereign country even if Russia finally capitulated and gave in. First, an independent Chechnya would be forced to deal with world sanctions—including the prosecution of its leadership for human rights violations at the International Criminal Court, even if these same leaders emerge as the official leaders of the new nation. If they attempt to leave their country they should be hunted down, and any country harboring them would suffer sanctions and be isolated.

Refusing to recognize a country born out of terror, and prosecuting their leaders in international courts, might bring some reason, accountability, and restraint to terrorism. An unequivocal message would be sent that a legitimate country can no longer be born by illegitimate means. Yes, it often happened in the past—but in our new, more civilized and enlightened era, it is no longer acceptable.

Of course, this solution leaves many oppressed minorities without options, so as a corollary, it is vitally important to offer a legitimate alternative path to minority populations. For example, if a minority group within a country wishes to secede and can win a democratically conducted referendum for secession within its geographic boundaries, its wish should be honored. If the majority leadership of that country either refuses to conduct a referendum (supervised by a blue-ribbon international panel), or fails to act on the results, the consequences would be universal sanctions against that country.

This two-pronged solution—no recognition for countries that achieve independence through terror, while allowing for secession via a democratic vote—would force all sides in a conflict to use influence and political means rather than terror or oppression to achieve their goals. That is what we all should want.

> Conservative Muslims are scared to death that America is forcibly, permanently changing their way of life.

Change is inevitable, and peoples' changing aspirations or national identity need to be recognized one way or another. The solution is to legitimize change by providing legitimate means. People should not have to resort to terror to emancipate themselves.

Is this a realistic solution?

Yes, *if* the principles I've outlined are universally accepted and carried out in good faith, especially by all the major global powers.

Is that a reasonable expectation?

I realize that many countries will not agree to sign such a pact, fearing that some of their own minorities will try to secede. If Turkey agreed to participate, for example, the Kurds in Turkey would immediately vote for separation. In Spain, both the Catalans and the Basques might vote to secede. And the Russians would be forced to allow the Chechens to vote and secede peacefully. This kind of pact could open a can of worms that very few countries would find palatable. In other words, the legitimate solution might prove very unattractive to those in power.

On the other hand, sooner or later we will have to face and recognize the consequences of *not* offering a legitimate, peaceful, and democratic solution. We are bringing this disaster called terrorism upon ourselves. Currently, minority groups that seek emancipation have no choice but to use terror as the means to achieve their aspirations. So we all have to bite the bullet, because it is going to hit us one way or the other.

Cultural Causes

Beyond nationalistic aspirations, there is another, more complicated cause for terrorism, which also appears difficult, if not impossible, to solve, and it is cultural in nature.

We have come to accept that those who would terrorize the West hate Western civilization and particularly its leader, the United States. Only people who hate—and hate relentlessly—could conceive the 9/11 attacks in which thousands of civilians perished.

Psychologists tell us that anger is caused by fear, or is actually fear in disguise. If that is true, then hate must be extreme fear. Hate must be absolute panic.

What is this panic about?

I suggest that conservative Muslims are scared to death that America is forcibly, permanently changing their way of life: liberating their women to such an extent that it will eventually destroy the traditional structure of their families; introducing pornography (although what is pornography to them may look to us like a woman in a bikini); and offering innumerable other, virtually irresistible "evil" temptations.

In her article "Fern Holland's War" in the September 19, 2004, *New York Times Magazine*, Elizabeth Rubin described the conflict as it played out in the Iraqi town of Karbala:

> By February of this year, Ms. Holland was busy getting a women's center up and running. … [Holland] unloaded new computers and other fancy goods for the sole benefit of Karbala's women. … Why were the Americans spending their money in this way? In Friday sermons, clerics loyal to the young militant Muqtada al-Sadr spread rumors: "You know what the Americans are doing in these centers, my brothers? They are offering free abortions. You know what these Internet centers are doing? They are offering free porn to the students of the Hawza [the Shiite seminary]."

Conservative Muslims are fighting for their lives as they know and like them, against a country that threatens their way of life and value system and is clearly superior in military terms. They have to use anything that gives them some advantage, such as suicide attacks, justified and supported by a widespread religious extremism that we cannot begin to compete with.

To reduce the terror caused by this cultural panic, we must reduce the fear. We must stop promoting our own cultural agenda—which is tantamount to cultural colonialism.

The same holds for *political* colonialism. We must stop proselytizing the forms of democracy, such as multi-party elections, that weaken the central powers and allow terrorist cells to flourish. Instead, we must first promote the conditions necessary for democracy to emerge: a healthy middle class based on small, self-owned enterprises; literacy; freedom of the press; and government accountability. Once that is accomplished, we should encourage freedom of the judiciary system from political intervention or economic corruption.

> Conservative Muslims are scared to death that America is forcibly, permanently changing their way of life.

Then, the foundations will exist for a multi-party system. If democracy is forced into a country mechanistically—form without function—before the conditions necessary for its success have evolved organically, the newborn democracy will be just a sham, too weak to fight terrorists who might try to destabilize the country. We must hold off on multiple parties and multi-party elections; these are the *forms* of democracy, not its foundation.

Can this happen?

I am pessimistic. How can we stop the spread of DVDs or pictures over the Internet, both of which promote cultural colonialism? This threat to the old way of life is not only here to stay, it is accelerating and cannot be stopped. What about political colonialism? There is a chicken-and-egg problem here: How do you advance the growth of the conditions for a successful democracy in a non-democratic regime, as the above solution suggests?

We are stuck.

It appears that terrorism is here to stay for at least a bit longer. It is a manifestation of our cultural, religious, economic, and political disintegration. It is a macro-manifestation of the accelerated global rate of change. Since there is no easy solution, we will likely see many more terrorist disasters, some of which will make 9/11 pale by comparison.

But maybe that is how the cookie has to crumble for a solution to emerge. The situation must get much, much worse before it can get better. It has to be bad enough that all of those who are needed for the solution feel equally threatened and thus are forced to cooperate in the solution. All countries will have to get together and do something really drastic, such as delegitimizing terror as a means to political emancipation, and/or agreeing to intervene militarily in totalitarian countries that harbor terrorists, remaining in these countries at all costs until and unless democracy succeeds.

Drastic? No doubt, but terrorism is a drastic problem that calls for drastic measures.

FIGHTING TERRORISM:
A STRUCTURALIST APPROACH[1]

"FIGHTING terrorism," Shimon Peres once said, "is like eating soup with a fork."

This sentence begs the question: If the enemy is "soup," then why *are* we fighting it with a "fork"? In other words, we are using the wrong tools in this war. We need to take into account the enemy's methods of fighting and develop counter-methods that mimic them.

For example, we should have an intelligence unit whose job is to study the structure of Al-Qaeda, and we should use that information to get ourselves organized accordingly. Our current structure—comprising an army, a navy, and an air force—is the right structure for fighting another country that has an army, a navy, and an air force. Al-Qaeda has none of these.

If what I have read in the newspapers is accurate, Al-Qaeda's structure is rather loose. (Even if this is incorrect, my point is still valid: We should organize ourselves to reflect the way *they* are organized.) Al-Qaeda basically has three support structures, and the rest is a network. The support structures are: the *madrassas*, the schools where young children and other interested parties are indoctrinated in radical Islamic ideology; the military training camps, where recruits learn the techniques of terrorism; and the Internet, where they are alerted to calls to action and where essential information, such as how to assemble bombs, is readily available.

Analyzed using the Adizes code[2], it is a (PA) system—a very strict, inflexible interpretation of the Koran and *sharia*, strong on rules and discipline—that is delivered to and integrated with others by committed

[1] Adizes Insights, January 2010.

[2] The (PAEI) code argues that managing an organization well involves having competence in four specific tasks: (P)roducing, (A)dministrating, (E)ntrepreneuring, and (I)ntegrating. For more information on the (PAEI) code, see my book *Management/Mismanagement Styles* (Santa Barbara, CA: Adizes Institute Publications, 2004).

individuals who use their own creativity to determine how to reach and attract others: in other words, an (EI) delivery, strong on (E)ntrepreneurship and (I)ntegration.

Ironically, Al-Qaeda's system fits modern American management principles so closely that you would think Osama bin Laden had studied the American management gurus and deliberately set out to apply their methods: Al-Qaeda is united by a common mission and system of values; it gives its members the tools to do the job; and its network is flexible enough to deliver the mission successfully.

The United States, on the other hand, works in just the opposite way: We have an (EI) ideology (democracy) that we try to deliver in a (PA) mode (with a military organization). It is as if we are following the traditional management theory of control and command, which modern management gurus have long rejected.

STEP-BY-STEP APPROACH

> Al-Qaeda's system fits modern American management principles so closely that you would think Osama bin Laden had studied the American management gurus and deliberately set out to apply their methods.

Now let us assume that we are willing to structure ourselves to fight terrorism in a way that mimics their system. What would we do first? We could establish our own *madrassas*, which would teach the ideology of diversity and tolerance. We could also set up training camps for anti-terrorism. And we would need to develop a network of cells or individuals dedicated to our ideology and ready to die for the cause, as they are.

The Wahhabi Saudis have established thousands of *madrassas* that feed Al-Qaeda with new recruits. We need to establish ten times that number of schools, where we teach the modern tools for economic success as well as the benefits of diversity, and we should subsidize the students, like the Wahhabis do. At the same time, we need to aggressively close their *madrassas*, to dry up the swamp where the mosquitoes breed.

That is Step 1. Step 2 is to close their training camps. Here is Step 3: Our tech people must find a way to disrupt the terrorists' use of the Internet as a source of information and networking tool, either by purveying disinformation or by blocking access to it completely.

To sum up: We are trying to fight our war against terrorism, a modern phenomenon, by using an old, inadequate methodology. Fighting terrorists is not like fighting another country. To win this war, we will need a different system.

WHAT IS IT LIKE
TO BE THE PRESIDENT
OF A DEMOCRATIC COUNTRY?[1]

I have attempted to reorganize the executive branches of several democratic countries, to no avail. The organizational chart did not change.

Usually, the chart needed changing because the country had some problems or priorities that its government was not organized to deal with head-on.

Take, for instance, the drug problem in the United States. The drug czar, as he was called, was supposed to coordinate other ministries in the war against drugs. But he was a czar without soldiers. No officers or generals, no troops. Whatever he was able to accomplish, he got through hours of begging and pleading with other agencies.

In Montenegro, the Agency for Environmental Protection reports to the Ministry of Tourism. Currently the country is gung-ho on developing tourism. As a result, the environmental agency, which reports to people who are far more interested in development than in protection, is crippled. It's as if an organization's quality control department reported to production.

It is difficult, if not impossible, to change the structure of the executive branch because that structure is determined by law. In order to eliminate one ministry and establish another one, it is necessary to get approval from the legislative branch. This gets enormously complicated because of the political trading that determines who gets which position or ministry.

For example, to encourage a party to join a particular coalition, the coalition-builder may offer that party the leadership of, say, the Ministry of Economics. And when the leadership of ministries is allocated to political parties, internal party politics, rather than experience or merit, will determine who heads the ministry. Often, in fact, a person will be appointed

---

[1] Adizes Insights, February 2007.

who has no relevant background at all. Take Israel, for example: It once had a minister of defense who had zero experience in defense matters. He was actually a trade-union organizer.

Thus, trying to make any changes in ministries requires complicated political trades, which could destabilize the government or even cause the Cabinet to fall. Even the budgets of ministries are hostage to political horse-trading. In Israel, for instance, the religious parties always insist on heading the Ministry of the Interior, which determines citizenship and performs the gate-keeping function as to who is a Jew. In exchange for voting with the prime minister, they expect a significant budget allocation to their religious schools, even though that might not be the country's most important priority at the time.

How This Plays Out

Now: Watch the prime minister maneuver his agenda. The government is not structured to deliver his priorities; the budgets do not *reflect* his priorities; and the people who head the ministries do not necessarily have the skills to do their jobs.

On top of that, the ministers who belong to the opposition party are more loyal to their party than to the prime minister. And, of course, some of the ministers of the prime minister's *own* party are also rooting for his demise so that they can take over the leadership position.

> What I cannot understand is why any normal person would want to lead under these circumstances.

Under these circumstances, how motivated could you be to make hard decisions, and what chance do you have to see them through?

Here is one more barrier to your effectiveness as a leader: A major part of the government's budget goes to pay government employees, who are organized in strong trade unions that have a high percentage of active voters. If you try to enact any economic reform that threatens their share of the government pie, the trade unions will strike, the country will become paralyzed, and you will probably not be re-elected. (Here I am describing the situation in Brazil.)

What would you do? You would *act* as if you were in control and make lots of speeches—but no waves, right?

This was true of Vicente Fox's government in Mexico. When I consulted to Fox, I tried to give more power to law-and-order government agencies, because their power was practically non-existent. But creating such a structure required parliamentary approval, and Fox had no control of his own party, much less the Parliament.

Furthermore, the biggest chunk of the government budget went to education, which was, and still is, ineffective, outdated, and outlandishly expensive. So education had resources it wasted, while law and order was on an anorexic diet. But change cannot occur: The teachers' union is extremely powerful, and its members vote en masse.

So what happens? Beyond empty promises, nothing much.

I don't find it strange that people do not trust their political leaders. Why would they? They make promises, get elected, and then don't deliver.

What I cannot understand is why any normal person would want to lead under these circumstances.

The only explanation I can think of is that the potential leader's ego is so enormous that he becomes a prisoner of that ego and believes he can overcome the truly unmanageable. Or else, he goes into denial and acts like the emperor in the children's story "The Emperor's New Clothes": He pretends to lead and be powerful, while in reality everyone knows he is nude.

The Dangerous Imbalance[1]

SO many people young and old would like to make this a better world. But to change the world, it is not enough to be individually conscious. Here is why.

The business world, a sub-system of society, is a very well-oiled machine, developed over thousands of years. It has its capital markets (and global ones, at that), a stock market, a banking system, private equity funds, etc. So if you have a good, tested idea, you can get the capital to start a business and, later on, finance its expansion.

The business world has created programs to train its leadership: business schools, executive training, etc. It has measurements of success; it has the clarity of measurable goals. It has no shame or reluctance about getting into strategic alliances in order to grow further.

It is such a perfectly tooled, efficient machine that it has developed a life of its own, which is starting to endanger the natural environment—our air, water, and natural resources. It has such deep pockets that it disproportionately influences other segments of society, such as the political environment. And it impacts the social environment by causing deep disintegration—more differentiation between rich and poor, both within a country and globally. It affects everything: environment, politics, society, even the legal structure.

Now let's compare the "greens," those socially conscious people who are trying to reduce the speed with which the world is advancing to its demise. They are very weak. They have no capital markets; they are splintered and rarely cooperate because they compete for the same limited resources and volunteers. Many are managed by big egos. I sit at some meetings of those well-meaning organizations and I witness how feeble their strategic thinking is. They do have plenty of good intentions and a sincere willingness to make

---

[1] Adizes Insights, February 2006.

a better world, but when you compare that to the logic and sharp thinking of the business world, their powers pale in comparison.

These much-needed organizations have goals that are managerially inferior to those of the business world. Their goals are all "anti-": anti-pollution, anti-global warming, anti- this or that. It is much more difficult to manage and reach "anti-" goals than "pro-" goals, such as more market share or more profits. So members of these organizations end up chaining themselves to the gates of nuclear facilities or burning down McDonald's restaurants in their frustration and eagerness to make a change.

This imbalance of power between business institutions and socially conscious institutions means to me that the stronger group will win—and we are marching to our demise.

Let me make one thing clear: I am not saying that businessmen are irresponsible and have no conscience. Many of them see that our world is "going south," and they join not-for-profits to try to change things.

The problem is not with people. It is with a system that is stronger than the people in it. We are still sitting in the driver's seat of the car, but increasingly, the car is really being driven by its automatic computer systems, and we are becoming mere passengers.

Unless …

Unless the non-governmental organizations (NGOs) get together and start cooperating on a global scale. *Unless* they develop their own competitive edge. *Unless* they unite.

If you count how many people are involved with NGOs globally, it is probably more than a billion—and yet their political influence does not reflect it.

THE SAD SIDE EFFECTS OF GLOBALIZATION[1]

I love folk music. From any country, from any ethnic group. I love the accordion. I play it, and it is my true vehicle for relaxation. Wherever I travel in the world, I try to find people singing their national or ethnic folk songs, or just join in some community singing.

But I can hardly find any. Of the fifty-two countries I have now visited, there are only three where you can still find a restaurant in which people eat and sing: Serbia, Portugal, and Mexico. (Maybe Greece, too, but I have not been there for a while and it might have changed.)

National songs are disappearing. I remember traveling for the first time to Peru. I was excited to be visiting a new culture. Arriving at the airport, I noticed that there was piped music playing over the PA system. I listened carefully, hoping to hear some local Peruvian music. They were playing "I Left My Heart in San Francisco."

In Moscow, I begged my hosts to take me to a place where I could listen to Russian songs or hear an accordion player. Nada. Nothing. You cannot find anyplace in Moscow where there is authentic accordion playing or people participating in sing-alongs. Instead, there are tourist traps where professional dancers and singers will perform some folk dances and a song or two. But you will never find locals there.

It was not always like this. In Macedonia, I remember, there were a number of restaurants where a quartet played national music for the guests, who would join the singing and even get up and dance a traditional dance or two between courses.

No more. If you want to see national dancing now, you have to ask if there is a wedding. They might dance there.

---

[1] Adizes Insights, June 2009.

I was recently in Paris. My dream was to go to a restaurant and hear French *chansons* and accordion playing. No way. I looked everywhere. I asked every concierge in the most expensive hotels. Nothing. "It used to be …" they told me. Apparently that charming tradition does not exist anymore. It was like going to the Sahara and not finding any sand.

I finally heard an accordion player in Paris—in a subway station. He was from Romania. I gave him my change.

> Local national cuisine is disappearing. … Fast food is taking over everywhere.

There are no more French accordion players. Can you believe that? Nor could I find any in Russia. One still can find a few in Italy, but they are old people. In the United States, it was almost impossible to find someone to repair my accordion. Finally in San Diego, I found an elderly Serbian man who could do it, and I sent him the accordion immediately, worrying that he might die before he fixed it.

National folk music and dances are speedily disappearing, replaced by generic pop music. Watching the local MTV in other countries is no different—in rhythm or presentation—from the one we see in the United States. Only the language is different. If I turned off the sound, I would not know which country I was in.

Fast-Food Globe

It is not only music and musical instruments that are disappearing. Local national cuisine is disappearing, too. Fast food is taking over everywhere. In addition to the McDonald's and Kentucky Fried Chickens, pizzas proliferate. The whole world is being invaded by cheap Italian cuisine. Why? Because it is inexpensive and easy to prepare, thus extremely profitable to serve.

Furthermore, the international cuisine we think we're eating in local restaurants is very different from the food you find in the countries themselves. For example, Turkish food served anywhere outside of Turkey is not at all the same food you would find *in* Turkey. It gets adapted to the local taste. In Mexico, you could not find easily, if at all, the Mexican food that is served in the United States. The pizza in Italy tastes nothing like the pizza you get at California Pizza Kitchen. National cuisines are disappearing, even though the names are kept.

National customs, music, food, dress, are all threatened with extinction. I see it in Macedonia. I see it in Montenegro. Three years ago, you could find many local restaurants with a "national kitchen." When I was there this past February, those same restaurants were serving pasta and steaks. That is what tourists want; that is what they get.

The big hotel chains look the same everywhere. The food is increasingly the same. I am starting to wonder where I am when I travel. We are losing our diversity. We should not allow that to happen.

In Mexico City, there is a restaurant, La Fonda del Recuerdo, that serves only traditional Mexican dishes, which they research and cook religiously according to the traditional recipe. The music played there is exclusively Mexican. You can feel that you are truly in Mexico.

Every country should do that. UNESCO has a system for protecting buildings and cities as part of mankind's heritage. France, Mexico, Italy, and Spain all applied to have their national cuisines recognized as "intangible" world heritage, and were rejected, because UNESCO has no category for gastronomy. How sad—and, may I add, how stupid. We need to protect more than rare plants and birds; we must also guard our customs, our songs, our music, and our food.

PART 2

CHALLENGES FOR COUNTRIES IN TRANSITION

RECOGNIZING REALITY
IN MACEDONIA[1]

FOR a long time I have been very pessimistic about Macedonia. Between 1993 and 1995, while consulting to Prime Minister Branko Crvenkovski there, I tried to persuade him to accept the notion of a multi-ethnic society. "It is inevitable anyway," I told him. "Over time, the Slavic Macedonians are bound to become a minority, because of the demographics of the Albanian Macedonians."

The same thing happened in Kosovo: In the 1940s there were only 40,000 Albanians in Kosovo; now there are two million. "We will win in bed!" went the well-known Kosovar war cry.

But ten years ago, a multi-ethnic society was unacceptable to Macedonians. They wanted a Macedonian state with an Albanian minority. Over and over again, I tried to explain that if Macedonia were located in Arizona, then the Albanians would be a national minority. But Macedonia is not in Arizona; it is in the heart of the Balkans, where, to the north, there are two million Albanians in Kosovo; to the west, in Albania, there are more than three million; and in Greece, to the south, there may be as many as 750,000 Albanians.

So who is the real minority? Turn on the television and surf the channels, and you can see for yourself who is in the minority and who is in the majority. Legal boundaries are weak arbiters of a state when travel, television, and telecommunications make those boundaries so porous. In those contexts, the Albanians are the largest population of southeastern Europe. (Same problem with the Arabs in Israel.)

During my visit there in November 2003, however, I saw a significant change. Prime Minister Crvenkovski is truly trying to promote a multi-ethnic

---

[1] Excerpted from Adizes Insights, November 2003.

society. One enormous step in the right direction was to approve as the country's official languages both Macedonian and Albanian. This means that school can now be taught in both languages, and that the Macedonian court system will also be bilingual.

This creates a lot of hardship for the Macedonians, who do not speak Albanian, while most Albanians do speak Macedonian. There is a similar state of affairs in Israel, where both Arabic and Hebrew are recognized languages but where Israelis do not generally learn to speak Arabic, while Arabs, the minority population, learn Hebrew in order to navigate the alien culture. If, in a courtroom, both the judge and the defendant's attorney are Arabs, and the prosecutor is Israeli, the Israeli will be at a disadvantage: When Arabic is being spoken she is out of the loop, while when she speaks Hebrew the other two understand what she is saying.

In both Macedonia and Israel, the disadvantage stems from the majority population's inability or unwillingness to recognize that they do, in fact, live in a multi-ethnic society. That recognition is not a matter of lip service, some kind of polite concession to the smaller segment of the population. It has consequences, which will become larger and more serious with time.

DEVELOPMENTAL CHALLENGES IN THE FORMER YUGOSLAVIA[1]

O N a business trip in 2006 that included stops in several countries that were once part of Yugoslavia, I saw a number of problems that need to be addressed. Here are my insights:

MONTENEGRO

I wrote to my wife: "I found the most beautiful country in the world [and I have worked and lectured in fifty-one so far]. It has the fjords of Norway, the warm water of Hawaii to swim in, the little romantic villages of Greece, the clean air of Switzerland, and fresh, fresh fruits and vegetables and grilled fish right out of the sea."

And guess what? It is about two hours from Frankfurt and an hour from Rome by air. It is in the center of Europe. Unspoiled.

How come we never hear about this country? Because until very recently it was part of Serbia, and Serbia has been ostracized by the world community for dozens of years.

Six months ago there was a Montenegrin referendum on the issue of whether to separate from the Serbian federation, and by a very small margin, the vote was for separation. Why the small margin? Because a large portion of the population is Serb. Why the vote to separate? I was told that Montenegrins were tired of being subservient to Belgrade. Everything needed permission from Belgrade. They wanted to have their fate in their own hands.

The new constitution has a paragraph declaring that Montenegro is and will always be an ecological state—which means no pollution of water, air, or land, and their agriculture will remain organic.

---

[1] Excerpted from Adizes Insights, September 2006.

But how successful will the government be in respecting that commitment? Money is pouring in, especially from Russia. The Russians are buying everything in sight. Hotels are being built everywhere. Roads are getting clogged. The highway from Slovenia to Croatia is so crowded with tourists already that there are reports of road rage and people stuck on highways for hours trying to get to their vacation spot.

Unfortunately, the structure of the executive branch is such that the administrative function is under production in the managerial hierarchy; for example, the Environment Protection Agency is part of the Ministry of Tourism, and the Agency for Spatial and Urban Planning reports to the Ministry of Economic Development. Thus, the administrative function, which sets rules and controls, is undermined.

Without strong controls, it is likely that development will overrun the place, ruining the country's chances for incredible success. Stay tuned.

SLOVENIA

In a survey in which people were asked whether they felt better off or worse after splitting from the Yugoslav federation … the majority felt they were better off during the federation.

Years ago there was a joke in Slovenia: The former president decided to scare the United States and sent a missile to destroy New York. Despite reports of major destruction, there was no response from the United States.

So he sent another missile, this time aimed at Washington, D.C. Destruction was reported, but again there was no response. He tried the third time against Los Angeles. Again no response.

Annoyed, he called Bill Clinton, who was the President of the United States at that time, and asked him: "How come you are not reacting?"

Clinton said, "I am going to severely punish you, as soon as I find you on the map. …"

It is a small country. It used to be part of Yugoslavia, but in 1991 it separated. It is south of Austria, east of Italy, and north of Croatia. It is beautiful: mountains, lakes, clean little villages like those in Austria. It is well managed: no corruption, no mafia managing the country from behind the scenes, as is the case in many countries in transition.

Interestingly, in a survey in which people were asked whether they felt better off or worse after splitting from the Yugoslav federation, the response was a surprise. The majority felt they were better off during the federation. Many have good memories of the Yugoslav federation. Yugoslavia meant something on the world scene. People felt proud to be Yugoslavs. It is interesting how important the emotional context is—far stronger and more important than the material economic context. I think the same is true for Bosnia and even Macedonia. Many now lament the split of the federation. Of course, there is no chance of turning back the wheels of history.

As each former republic of Yugoslavia joins the European community, the borders will become meaningless economically, as they will all be part of one economic market. In one sense, they will be together again, but the pride, the identity of Yugoslavia is lost forever.

The current president of Slovenia, who suffers from cancer, experienced a spiritual awakening and sees himself as responsible not only for Slovenia but for humanity in general. He is trying to play a role in the Middle East and to help stop the genocide in Darfur.

Hmm. … Maybe a condition for electing all politicians should be that they have survived some serious, life-threatening disease. Maybe then they could be trusted.

MEXICO'S SORRY PRESIDENTIAL POLITICS[1]

WHEN Vicente Fox was elected president six years ago, I did some work with him during the transition period. I organized Los Pinos, which is the equivalent of the White House in the United States, and organized the executive branch along the (PAEI) model.[2]

It is no secret that Fox came to power through direct elections by the people. His own party did not fully support him, and he had no control of the Parliament, either. Just to show you how weak he was from the start of his administration, when he flew to visit one Latin American country, the chairman of his own party, PAN, refused to fly with him on the presidential plane and flew separately.

Fox was a lame duck from his first day as president. But he also contributed to his own weakness. When I asked him what his main agenda was, he answered that it was to democratize the presidency, which till then had been very "imperial": The president was all-powerful, even appointing his own successor, so elections were more a ritual than anything substantive. So, Fox did not have the votes in the Parliament to start with, and because of his agenda, he did not work on strengthening his position, either. As a result, he could not lead.

FOLLOWING IN GORBACHEV'S PATH

I told Fox that he was repeating Mikhail Gorbachev's mistake. I had written an analysis for Gorbachev back when he was *Time* magazine's "Man of

---

[1] Excerpted from Adizes Insights, September 2006.

[2] The (PAEI) code argues that managing an organization well involves having competence in four specific tasks: (P)roducing, (A)dministrating, (E)ntrepreneuring, and (I)ntegrating. For more information on the (PAEI) code, see my book *Management/Mismanagement Styles* (Santa Barbara, CA: Adizes Institute Publications, 2004).

the Year," in 1987.[3] In that paper, I pointed out that his methods in changing the Soviet system were incorrectly applied. *Perestroika* (economic, political, and social restructuring) requires political strength. *Glasnost* (political openness) weakens political power. Since economic restructuring requires political strength, he should have started with *perestroika* and then slowly followed it with *glasnost*, the way the Chinese are doing now, rather than starting with *glasnost*, losing power, and thus being unable to deliver the *perestroika*. He would lose his power, I predicted, and the system would collapse—as it did.

I do not think Gorbachev ever read my paper, although I sent it through his economic advisor. In the case of Fox, I told him during a dinner, attended by just the two of us, that he should not fight the "imperial" presidency because he was going to need that power to make the changes the country needed. Property rights, for example, had been totally messed up by Luis Echeverría, one of his predecessors, who had redistributed private land to the peasants.

Furthermore, Mexico has a serious problem in its education system, and the disparity between the "haves" and "have-nots" is extreme. Making changes in these areas requires political power, so the last thing Fox should have done was to diminish the limited power he had.

But for whatever reason, he did not follow that advice.

With the most recent elections, in 2006, his weakness was actually embarrassing. Felipe Calderón, from Fox's own party, was elected, but by an extremely small margin. His opponent, Andrés Manuel López Obrador, is contesting the election, even though the electoral college has already recounted some disputed stations and announced Calderón as the winner. Obrador, or AMLO as he is called for short, is challenging not only Calderón, the new president, but also Fox, the sitting president.

> *Vicente Fox was a lame duck from his first day as president. But he also contributed to his own weakness.*

Fox could not even deliver his State of the Union speech before Parliament, because members of AMLO's party took over the podium and prevented him from speaking. On Mexico's Independence Day, it is traditional for the president to kick off the celebrations by shouting *"El Grito!"*—the cry for

---

[3] Gorbachev was also *Time* magazine's "Man of the Decade" in 1989.

independence, recalling the *grito* (or cry) that started the revolution. It is done from a particular balcony overlooking the main square in Mexico City, the Zocalo. Well, not this year. AMLO's supporters blocked the square, and President Fox had to move his *grito* to another balcony in another city.

This is more than embarrassing.

AMLO refuses to recognize the validity of the elections, and has announced an alternative presidency. He is planning mass disobedience, which might mean refusing to pay taxes, blocking main transportation arteries, etc.

And Fox is doing nothing. He is still the president, but a very, very weak one, and a lame duck, too.

Development and
the Quality of Life[1]

YOU would expect that the more effective you are, the more problems you will solve and thus the fewer problems you will have. Right?

Wrong.

In reality, the more problems you solve, the more problems you will have; and the faster you solve them, the faster new ones will emerge.

Conclusion: The more effective you are, the more ineffective you will feel.

How come? What is going on?

We all know that change is constant: It has been going on forever, and it will continue forever. Whenever there is change, there is, by definition, a new event. That event can be either a problem or an opportunity. I call it an "oppor-threat," because every problem is a de facto opportunity to improve your know-how—if it is handled correctly.

On the other hand, an event that seems like an opportunity might turn out to be a real problem if you mishandle it. Thus, an event is initially both a problem and an opportunity. What it turns out to be depends on what you do with it.

The point I want to make, however, is that regardless of whether the event is a problem or an opportunity, it needs to be handled. It needs to be addressed. We must decide what to do and then implement that decision. When we act in response to the event, once we make a decision and implement that decision, our action has caused a change. Now we have a new situation, which creates new problems. That is why problems will be here to stay forever, as long as there is change.

But something interesting is happening that leads me to write this Insight:

---

[1] Adizes Insights, January 2007.

Imagine that devices and/or managerial tools have been developed that enable you to diagnose a problem faster, make your decision faster, and implement your decision faster. That sounds good, does it not?

You can address the problem promptly and deal with it promptly. But that means that you will also create a new situation just as promptly—a change that will bring new problems to your plate—because the faster we solve problems, the faster the new ones will appear.

Take e-mail, for instance. It was supposed to facilitate faster, paperless communication and thus make us more effective. And what happened? I, for one, have many more problems to deal with than I had before the innovation of e-mail. The more effective we are, the faster we advance, and the faster new problems confront us.

THE PRICE OF DEVELOPMENT

The more developed the country is, the more smoothly things get done; thus the faster new problems appear; thus the more stressed people are.

When I work in a developing country, nothing works easily and smoothly. It is difficult to get a phone connection; transportation is not reliable; there is lots of waiting around for everything to happen. It is ineffective and inefficient, but guess what? People have smiles on their faces. They have time to talk to me and to each other. People are less stressed; they take problems in stride. In underdeveloped nations, the normal reaction to an emerging need to solve a problem is, "*Mañana.*" Tomorrow. People are poor but happy, while in developed countries they are rich and miserable.

I grasped this insight from my travels. I noticed that the more developed the country was, the more stressed its citizens were. The enormous stress is a consequence of the accelerating rate of emerging problems that develop as the country becomes more efficient. As it becomes more efficient, it can afford to be more effective, i.e., solve more and more problems. But the more problems it solves, the more new ones emerge.

Here is an example: Recently I traveled to the Albanian capital city of Tirana. It was around midnight by the time I arrived at the hotel, and I was hungry, but there was no room service there. So I asked the driver where I could eat that late at night. He pointed down the road and said there was a pizzeria there, open all night long.

I looked in the direction he pointed. It was a dark alley. It was late. I was sure I would be killed or at least robbed, so I asked him if it was dangerous. He looked at me, bewildered. "Why?" he asked.

"Don't you have crime in this city?" I asked.

To my surprise, I found out that the crime rate in Albania is quite low. No serious crimes. It is safe to walk the streets. The streets are dark all night long, but even women can walk there without worry.

What is going on? This is a poor country, and don't poor people frequently rob others?

No. This experience confirmed my theory that crime is not caused by poverty but is, rather, a manifestation of disintegration. There is crime in Mexico City. You cannot walk at night in Sao Paulo, Brazil. This is because the difference between the rich and the poor is staggering in these countries.

But this disintegration has not yet reached Albania. As yet, *everyone* is somewhat poor there. You will not find much crime in poor villages anywhere in the world. By contrast, the rich people of Mexico and Brazil cannot go to a restaurant without bodyguards. Their children are taken to school in armored cars. And they spend their vacations out of their country, where no one knows them.

As we develop on one hand, we disintegrate on the other—whether it is in our personal lives, our companies, our countries, or globally.[2]

DEVELOPMENT: DREAM OR NIGHTMARE?

In December 2006, I diagnosed the problems of a new country—Montenegro—with its whole Cabinet in attendance. We analyzed what issues the country was currently facing, as well as its vision for the future. And as expected, they are moving full speed ahead toward development; they all want to be like "America." Notice that I put "America" in quotation marks, to indicate that it is less a geographical location than the ideal, or myth, of an efficiently running country, with highways, an excellent banking system, a developed IT infrastructure, etc.

To truly become a developed country looks to the Montenegrins like a dream. But to me, who has experienced this dream, it is more like a

---

[2] Excerpted from Adizes Insights, February 2006.

nightmare. Right now in Montenegro, friends meet at least once a week and drop in at each other's homes without announcing their intentions in advance. At least once a month they get together to celebrate something, a birthday or anniversary or some religious holiday. And they have time for community singing and for eating "slow food" rather than "fast food." The restaurants are filled with people drinking, talking, laughing (and, unfortunately, smoking).

Where I live in California, best friends get together at best once a month; communication is more by e-mail and phone than face-to-face; and no one would dare to show up at my home unannounced. The get-togethers are scheduled months in advance. The same even holds true for my 12-year-old son. He does not go out to the street and play with his friends like I did. Instead, a play date has to be scheduled in advance, and he has to be driven back and forth, monitored and supervised.

> *In a developed country ... the standard of living is higher but the quality of life is lower.*

In a developed country, in other words, the standard of living is higher but the quality of life is lower. In developing countries the situation is reversed: The standard of living is lower, but the quality of life is higher. Family and friends are truly valued, and people have time for themselves and for each other.

I told the government of Montenegro that in my humble opinion they should not encourage investments too fast. If they aren't careful, I said, "You will destroy this beautiful country in no time. Your problem is not how to encourage investments but how to discourage the bad investments." For that, Montenegro needs to have a conceptual plan that outlines what it wants to be.

"Your roads are already clogged," I continued. "So what will you do? Expand them? How? You will need about ten lanes, like in Los Angeles, to accommodate all the tourism you are encouraging. And would even *that* stop the bumper-to-bumper traffic?"

What they want to avoid at all costs, I said, is the fate of Acapulco and, soon, Cancun, where over-expansion has destroyed the natural beauty of the place.

My recommendation was to skip development: Small is beautiful; underdeveloped is beautiful, too. No big hotels, I told them; just small bed-and-breakfast inns. And keep the national cuisine alive. Prohibit the fast-food chains from establishing themselves in the country. Slow down.

In fact, "Slow down" was my slogan. Do not develop. Protect what you have. Make your disadvantage into an advantage. Make lemonade out of a lemon. Keep your underdeveloped country protected from development. (Imagine: The people of Montenegro can still drink water directly from the flowing river. Where else can you do that?)

But I doubt there is any chance my recommendations will be accepted. I tried the same thing in Macedonia years ago. No one would listen. People feel that they will be left behind, that they are missing the good life, with the big department stores and the enormous range of choices one is exposed to. It is only after they experience the disintegration, the alienation, and the stress that inevitably accompanies development that they decide to pull back and slow down. But by then, of course, the rivers have been polluted and the air is dangerous to breathe. Time flies, and there is no time for anything. Life is short because it is too fast, and it is too fast because we have made our world too efficient.

My conclusion is that we pay a high personal price for being more efficient and effective. To overcome this difficulty, in developed countries we would have to acquire the discipline to decide that it's OK to live without solving every problem on the table. We would have to learn to prioritize. In other words, *we* have to take control of our lives and problems, instead of letting the *problems* take control of our lives.

TURKEY'S EVOLVING CONSTITUTION[1]

M Y trip in September and October 2007 was one of the longest and most tiring I have ever taken. It started with a week in Istanbul, Turkey. Here are my impressions:

BALANCING RELIGION AND SECULARITY

In Turkey, I met with an advisor to the prime minister. I asked him what issues the prime minister is mainly preoccupied with. He said: "The Constitution."

Turkey is in the midst of changing some parts of its Constitution. What is at stake, according to this advisor, is the role the military plays in managing the affairs of the state. As we know, in Turkey the military is given the role of protecting the state from religious interference. The current prime minister comes from a Muslim religious party, and the country has been struggling to find the right balance between religion and secularity—between what the government, led by a religious party, wants, and what the military wants.

For instance, there is a debate about whether women can wear a head scarf to school or not. Another question is whether the Kurdish language should be recognized as one of the country's official languages.

What became apparent to me during this conversation was that the prime minister is attempting to use Turkey's application to enter the European Union as a way to reduce the power of the military, and thus increase the power of the political establishment, led at present by the religious Muslim party he heads.

How?

The European Union has rules and guidelines, and one of them is that

---

[1] Excerpted from Adizes Insights, October 2007.

the military should not have a voice in politics. So the EU insists on reducing the power of the military in Turkey.

If I am right, the EU might have a dilemma: It wants a non-military-dominated democracy, but in Turkey this will result in a strong Muslim-led government.

For democracy to be workable in function as well as in form, no single interested institution should get hold of political power—not the military and not the religious parties, either. But that is what is happening in Turkey and virtually in Israel, too, where the minority religious parties can make or break governments.

> For democracy to be workable in function as well as in form, no single interested institution should get hold of political power—not the military and not the religious parties, either.

Nor should the government be colluding with powerful businesses, as in Serbia today, where members of the Cabinet also sit on the boards of directors of major companies; or in the United States, where the political left is claiming that big business dominates the political agenda.

Any collusion of powerful interests with government is undesirable. Ideally, the military *should* be out of government. But religion and business should be out of government, too. Maybe even Socrates was wrong when he said countries should be governed by "philosopher/kings." Philosophers are just as biased as the others.

Democracy, by definition, means no monopoly or even oligopoly of powers; multiple powers—none dominant—seems to be the answer. The role of a political leader, then, is not to represent any single point of view but to integrate different points of view.

PROHIBITING INTIMIDATION

As for the issues themselves, I told the prime minister's advisor that, based on the principles of mutual trust and respect, I see no reason why women cannot wear head scarves to cover their hair.

The problem, however, as discussed at length in the media, is what they call "neighborhood pressure." The fear is that, if permitted, those who do wear scarves are going to put social pressure on those who prefer not to wear them.

I told the advisor that I wondered if the solution, based on mutual trust and respect, is not to prohibit scarves, but to prohibit intimidation. Just as sexual harassment is prohibited, so should religious harassment be prohibited. Both parties should recognize each other's undeniable right to follow whatever behavior suits their beliefs as long as it does not interfere with other people's beliefs.

As I have said in many of my lectures: "I do not care what you think of me. I do not care if you do not respect me. Just *behave* as if you do. God apparently did not want us to know what other people think. If S/He did, S/He would have put a video screen on everybody's forehead. You can think whatever you want, as long as you do not behave in a way that prohibits me from thinking whatever I want. What counts is not what you *think* but what you *do*."

So wear scarves if that makes you feel good. Just do not force the scarf on me. And the reverse is also true: If you do not want to wear a scarf, don't. But do not prohibit me from wearing one if I want to.

Mutual respect is a guideline for the solution. It seems simple but is difficult to implement because of problems of *trust*. Mutual trust means: If I let you behave in a certain way, would you reciprocate and let me be free to behave in *my* own way?

This experience reinforces my claim, debated at numerous Adizes conventions, that trust must precede respect. If there is no trust, respect cannot even start to influence the decisions being made.

WHAT'S WRONG WITH MULTIPLE LANGUAGES?

Whether to accept the Kurdish language as an official national language is a different problem. Many other countries, such as Montenegro, Macedonia, Israel, and even the United States have a similar issue: Should they recognize more than one language as a formal language of the country?

Based, again, on mutual trust and respect, I suggested that the issue is not how many languages a country recognizes as official. Granted, having two languages is more expensive, because court and other documents must be written in both languages, but that is the minor issue. The critical issue is how to avoid the disintegration of the country: If there are two formal languages, but they are not both spoken fluently by the entire population, that can lead to disintegration.

Two examples of such disintegration are Israel and Macedonia. The Arabs in Israel study Hebrew at school and speak it, but among themselves they speak only Arabic. The Jews, on the other hand, study Arabic very superficially and cannot really communicate in it; among themselves they speak Hebrew.

The Macedonians speak Macedonian, but the Albanians who live in Macedonia refuse to speak Macedonian, as a political statement.

That is also the danger in the United States: If Spanish becomes a second formal language, the Spanish-speaking people will not need to learn English anymore, and most English-speaking people will not know Spanish. Without a common language, we will have two nations sharing the same country, but unable to communicate without interpreters. It does not feel right, does it? I call that disintegration.

In Turkey, Macedonia, and Israel, my advice was the same: Two formal languages? Fine, but then the entire population *must be fluent* in both. This is how Switzerland operates: When a person from a French canton travels to a German canton, she speaks German.

Another solution is to choose English as the formal language that everyone must know, as Singapore did.

Whenever there is a danger of disintegration, we must legislate the antidote—integration—or the country risks being seriously damaged in the long run.

DEMOGRAPHIC ARITHMETIC IN MONTENEGRO[1]

IN Montenegro, I lectured to government administrators and under-secretaries of various ministries. Some of them enthusiastically told me that Montenegro today has a very positive balance of payments and a large surplus in the Treasury. They were proud of the foreign "investments" that are flooding the country.

I did not see it that way. In my view, they have a surplus only because they are selling off the country. Land, factories, buildings: Everything is for sale, and other nations, especially the Russians, are buying it all. "These are not investments," I said to the deputy prime minister when we had dinner together. "What will you sell when you have nothing left to sell?"

The country has gone big-time into tourism, planning to develop hotels with 35,000 additional beds—about 20,000 new rooms. "Where is the labor force going to come from?" I asked—a question I have asked on every visit. Let us not forget that Montenegro has only about 600,000 inhabitants. Its work force is about 200,000, most of them peasants or government bureaucrats. Obviously, workers will have to come from neighboring countries where the standard of living is even lower, such as Albania and Bosnia, and maybe even the unskilled workers of Serbia.

"So what? That's not a terrible thing," was the response. "Even now, we have a large Albanian minority. Ulcinj, one of the towns, is almost 100 percent Albanian."

"I am not anti-Albanian," I explained. "But will the foreign workers be citizens, with all the rights of citizenship? Or will it be like South Africa, where they brought in Africans to work in their mines and put them in

[1] Excerpted from Adizes Insights, October 2007.

90

shacks outside the city, treating them worse than second-class citizens? That is not a sustainable solution."

WHEN 'TEMPORARY' ISN'T TEMPORARY

It is never wise to apply a temporary solution to a permanent problem (or, for that matter, a permanent solution to a temporary problem). The need for a labor force in a massive, labor-intensive industry is a permanent problem; thus you need a permanent solution, not a temporary one.

Temporary solutions, if they do not change over time, become de facto permanent solutions by default. But they are probably the wrong solutions for the long run, because they were designed to work only as temporary, stopgap solutions.

> It is never wise to apply a temporary solution to a permanent problem (or, for that matter, a permanent solution to a temporary problem).

Look at what is happening in the United States, with twelve million non-legitimate workers. We need them to support our economy, but we don't want to recognize them as legitimate citizens. Because they are not legitimate citizens, they do not pay taxes, even though they use our health and educational resources. But if they were allowed to become citizens and vote, it would change the demographics of the country.

"In your case," I told the deputy prime minister, "if the enormous labor force you will have to import becomes legitimized, the original Montenegrins will become a minority in their own country."

The demographics of Montenegro are already problematic: The Parliament has been unable to approve the Constitution because they cannot agree on an official language: Should it be Serbian (Montenegro has a large Serb population) or Montenegrin?

"What will you do," I asked, "when your demographics change even more?"

As a new country, Montenegro has nationalistic aspirations. They want anything official to be uniquely Montenegrin. They have even formed a brand-new Montenegrin Orthodox church. (In the past, Montenegrins worshiped in a Serbian Orthodox church.)

It is not possible to remain uniquely Montenegrin, *and* absorb large populations from neighboring countries. A multi-ethnic country should be designed consciously—meaning that the Constitution has to reflect that. For example, the separation of state and religion must be stipulated, because different ethnic groups follow different religions.

The Montenegrins want to have their cake and eat it, too. But as we all know, that does not work.

THE PROBLEM OF
RAMPANT CORRUPTION

SERBIA[1]

WHEN Prime Minister Zoran Djindjic was murdered last March[2], I really believed that the long-term clash of power between the Serbian government and the powerful mafias would finally be resolved. The assassination, I thought, would at least serve as an effective pretext for the government to lock the mafia in prison, eliminate its power base, and take full power.

This clash of government and mafia is not unique to Yugoslavia. When the Communist regimes collapsed in Russia, Hungary, and elsewhere, and new democratic institutions did not immediately assume control, the mafia walked into those power vacuums, too.

In Russia, Vladimir Putin is trying hard to control the mafia and gain control for the legitimate government. And that is what should have happened in Yugoslavia.

The mafia had protected and supported Djindjic in his battle for power against Milosevic. But when he came to power, Djindjic did not return the favor. Not only did he refuse to allow the mafia to dictate any of his policies, but his administration began offering better protection to people who could testify against mafia members in court.

So the mafia killed him—or so I believe.[3] At the time, I also believed that Djindjic's assassination was such an outrage that his successor would

---

[1] Section on Serbia excerpted from Adizes Insights, November 2003.

[2] Djindjic was assassinated March 12, 2003.

[3] A decision in May 2007 by the Special Court for Organized Crime, in Belgrade, confirmed my suspicion, convicting twelve men, including members of the secret police and mafia kingpins, of Djindjic's murder.

finally have the will, the justification, and the force to end this unholy alliance between the mafia and the government. Finally, the mafia's power and influence in Yugoslavia could be reduced if not erased.

I was wrong. That is not what happened. The mafia was deeply engaged not only with Djinjdic but also with other government functionaries. And it is beginning to look as if Djindjic's own government wanted him gone as much as the mafia did.

As a result, Yugoslavia's privatization process is in fact a fixed game, in which those with government and mafia connections get what they want at the cheapest price, and everybody else loses. There is a bitter joke among the Serbs: "Some countries have a mafia. In Serbia, the mafia has a country."

The country is on its knees, although it's easy to be fooled by the busy, crowded restaurants. But in Serbia, restaurants play a therapeutic role. The more pain and tension people feel, the quicker they head to the neighborhood restaurant for some drinks and a heavy meal.

UKRAINE[4]

Which corrupt behavior is an accepted behavior depends partly on how long the behavior has been practiced, how openly it is practiced, and what is done about it, if anything.

I found that in Ukraine, businesses routinely pay "protection" money to a clandestine organization, which then guarantees that the business will not be audited by the tax authorities.

This is a widespread practice. It is not even a secret. When I showed total surprise, I was told that bribery is normal. A student can bribe a professor to give her a passing grade even if she never attended classes or took an exam. Some of the "attorneys" now practicing law, I was told, never actually studied it, and the same goes for some "doctors." They *bought* the diplomas. It's hard to believe, but I was assured that "everything is for sale," from a driver's license to the top political positions. It is only a question of price.

How does one eradicate this kind of corruption? Economic policy cannot be successful under those conditions—although it's true that people *do* adapt and work around or with a system, no matter how screwed up it is.

---

[4] Section on Ukraine excerpted from Adizes Insights, October 2007.

But without adequate taxation, how does the state provide such services as education and health? Clearly, inadequately. Those who have money buy those services privately or go abroad; while those who do not have money suffer and die. How long will people tolerate such a system before they start to cause turmoil or even a revolution?

VALUES PRECEDE FORM AND FUNCTION

There is form and there is function. But there are also the values upon which form and function are based.

Countries in transition often try to copy the United States' democratic system and its market economy. But their value systems may be different. The American system is based on fairness. People from other countries don't always understand this fair-play cultural doctrine. In fact, many interpret the Americans' assumption of fairness as being naïve or even stupid; I have heard this said more than once.

And why are Americans accused of being naïve? Because they believe what others tell them, and because the American systems of government and business give people unprecedented freedom to act, based on trust.

Here is a personal example, which surprised me when I first arrived in America: If you call the phone company and tell them that you put a quarter in the public phone box but did not get a connection, the phone company asks for your address and sends you a quarter. I was more than surprised when I experienced it myself. "The phone company believes what I say?" I wondered in total astonishment.

It's hard to believe, but I was assured that "everything is for sale," from a driver's license to the top political positions. It is only a question of price.

Or how about newspaper stands? You put money in and you are supposed to take only *one* newspaper out. They trust people not to steal and resell the newspapers. That would not happen in any of the countries I come from. There is no trust in any of them. In Russia during the Communist era, for example, you could not order a sandwich and then pay for it. No way. First you had to pay. Then, you got a ticket to pick up your sandwich.

So the U.S. market economy is free, true, but there are established values of what is fair, and if those values are violated, the government steps in. I notice this "fair-play" value system everywhere: in the park, in AYSO soccer games, in restaurants, waiting in line to board a plane—everywhere. The problem is that in some cultures that want to copy America's free-market model, fairness is hardly a cornerstone. *Their* value system is based on power: "Power talks." "Get power and use it to benefit yourself." And the ones who cannot get it or do not have it must live with the consequences. In those cultures, playing fair is for wimps.

The bottom line is that if countries try to duplicate the U.S. political and economic models but do not share the American value system, the result is a farce of American-style market openness in which those who have power enjoy obscene benefits, while those who have no power get, at best, crumbs. The combination of American economic and political models, plus a power-based value system, can create sociopolitical results that the Americans who exported the system would abhor.

PUTIN'S PREDICTABLE RELAPSE[1]

I N Belorussia, I watched the CNN program *Czar Putin,*[2] which argued that Vladimir Putin is destroying Russia's budding democracy. If I had watched the program from my bed in Santa Barbara, California, I believe I would have accepted that criticism of Putin, but watching it from Minsk, Belorussia, I had a different experience.

Why are people surprised at what Putin is doing?

Change is not linear. It is always two steps forward, one step back. Even in dieting that is true. There is always a relapse. No change advances forward in a straight line. And that is true especially for Russia, which has never, *ever*, had experience with democracy. The country has always moved from one dictatorship to another.

In this century, they have tried something completely different, and Russia has gone through remarkable changes, moving away from central planning and trying to adopt a market economy.

When we try to decentralize a company, much less a country, there are enormous reactions to, and problems with, cultural change. And here we are talking about a *country*—one of the largest on earth—which moved from government-owned to privately owned industry, from Communism to capitalism. This is not just a change of ownership. It is a change of an entire *values system*. The country could not make those changes without some relapses. That is normal.

Furthermore, Russia has traditionally not only accepted authority, it has *glorified* authority. That is how Stalin survived in power for so long. Those who went against this culture, like Boris Yeltsin, were and are despised. Yeltsin drank in public and danced like a circus clown. He broke apart the Soviet Union and is considered to be the leader who destroyed Russia's former

---

[1] From Adizes Insights, January 2008.

[2] Aired December 2, 2007.

glory. Putin, on the other hand, is perceived by many as the person who is bringing pride and self-respect back to Russia.

The accusation that Russia cannot have democracy without a robust opposition party is not relevant in Russia's present culture. An opposition party that criticizes Russian policies would be perceived as trying to weaken Russia, and Russians feel they have been weakened enough. They need to feel stronger now.

'FREEDOM SHOCK'

We are expecting Russians to adopt an *adversary* democracy, when in their current stage of cultural evolution, with their long history of glorifying authority, adversary relations naturally feel inauthentic to them. This is a phenomenon I learned about in Israel: The Russian Jews who immigrated to Israel between the 1970s and the 1990s experienced what sociologists called "freedom shock." They could not believe that people could criticize, make fun of, and put down Israel's elected leaders. To them, it seemed like spitting at your own mother.

> Russia has traditionally not only accepted authority, it has glorified authority.

We must realize that political systems do not comprise only voting regulations. They have a cultural component, and what is culturally acceptable to us can be totally alien to another country.

Another point: American newspapers criticize Putin for giving us a hard time about Iran and Kosovo. How strange! What did *we* do in 1962 when the Russians were going to put missiles in Cuba? We were ready to go to war. And now, President George W. Bush is putting missiles on the immediate borders of Russia, and yet we expect Putin to accept that lying down. How arrogant that is.

I am not defending Putin's actions here. Not at all. But what he is doing was to be expected. If it wasn't Putin, it would have been someone else doing the same thing. Putin is enacting a scenario that the country needs to play out; he is responding to Russian society's need to regain its footing, because the change it experienced was enormously disruptive.

The changes in Russia are immense, and Russia needs to stabilize before further democratization can occur. And when it does, this democratization will have to be internally driven rather than promoted by the United

States—otherwise the change will be perceived as being manipulated by foreign interests.

First, Russia must regain the pride it lost with the breakdown of the Soviet Union. Then, it must learn to control the vulgar capitalism that has become a runaway train. You see this in Moscow: People are begging across the street from an exhibition exclusively for millionaires, endorsing the worst kind of conspicuous consumption. People have not forgotten some of the aspirations of socialism; so far, they are suffering the income disparities quietly, but I don't believe they will continue to do that for much longer.

As in therapy, the corrective actions after the relapses have to come from the inside. They cannot be driven by someone else; that would only retard the evolution that will occur anyway, in time.

Kosovo Independence:
A Lucky 'Tragedy' for Serbia[1]

THERE are very, very few locations in the world that evoke as strong an emotional response as Kosovo does for the Serbs. It is like Jerusalem for the Jews, or Mecca for the Muslims.

It is difficult for Americans to understand this emotional connection, because there is no place in the United States, at least that I know of, that is worshiped, written about, and sung about like Kosovo.

For the Serbs, Kosovo is a powerful symbol of national unity. It is where they lost the war against the Turks and were enslaved for 500 years. It is where the Serb nation was "born." Kosovo has been celebrated by Serbs in their poetry, their music, and their art. Serbian children learn, starting in kindergarten, who died in Kosovo 500 years ago, and how.

Symbols can have profound, frequently irrational effects on people's emotions and their souls. Symbols can be dangerous. People will die for a symbol. They will send their children to die for a symbol.

Imagine what would happen if the Israelis were forced to give up the Western Wall. "It is only a wall," some people would argue. But that's irrelevant, because the Wall symbolizes the dreams and longings of the Jewish people for freedom and a homeland. I guarantee that blood would flow and people would die for that Wall.

What about Mecca? What would happen if the United States decided to recognize an independent Mecca, separate from the Muslim world? Can you imagine how the Muslim countries and individual Muslims would react?

Here's a hypothetical scenario that's closer to home: Imagine that Iran invaded the Statue of Liberty, occupied it, and claimed it as a Muslim shrine. How would the American people feel?

---

[1] Adizes Insights, February 2008.

Now multiply that emotional reaction a hundred or even a thousand times, and you might get an idea how the Serbs feel about losing Kosovo. It is their Serbian Jerusalem, their Mecca, their Statue of Liberty and Gettysburg and Alamo and Liberty Bell put together.

So, if it is so important to them, how did Serbia lose Kosovo?

It did not just happen on Sunday morning, February 17, 2008; Kosovo's declaration of independence was only the latest act in a drama that began a long time ago.

In 1991, when the prime minister of Serbia asked me to consult to his government about the breakup of the Yugoslav federation, I learned the following:

At the end of World War II, the Albanians in Kosovo comprised less than a hundred thousand souls. But their rate of reproduction is one of the highest in the world—about nine children per family, if I am not mistaken. So over the years, they multiplied, until today they are two million people. According to a report by the Helsinki Committee for Human Rights in Serbia, Albanians bought land in Kosovo by terrorizing the local Serbs into selling to them.

MILOSEVIC'S CAMPAIGN PROMISES

Slobodan Milosevic came to power in 1986. His campaign motto was "Kosovo to Serbia," which stressed his intention to regain Kosovo, Serbia's "national cradle," for the Serbs. During his campaign, a million people marched in Belgrade to demonstrate support for him, and he was elected to the presidency.

Earlier, when Josep Broz Tito was in power, every republic in the Yugoslav federation was required to allocate funds to support the developing part of Yugoslavia—a.k.a. Kosovo. Kosovo was then, and still is, underdeveloped, a problem that is compounded by its soaring birth rate and widespread unemployment.

Under Tito's heavy hand, no one dared to challenge this policy. But after his death, as the Committee of Presidents that ruled Yugoslavia became politically weaker and weaker, the Croats and Slovenes challenged the policy.

The Slovenes do not share a religion, a culture, or even a language with

Serbia. "Why are we supporting the cradle of the Serbian nation?" they wanted to know.

The Croats, who are Catholics (the Serbs are Christian Orthodox), did not want to support Muslim Kosovo financially, either. "If it is the cradle of the Serb nation, let *them* pay for it," was their attitude.

Both Slovenia and Croatia had been dreaming of independence for centuries. So when Milosevic unilaterally raided the Yugoslav federal treasury for funds to prop up Kosovo, he gave both countries a good excuse to leave the federation. "We refuse to be dominated by Serbia; we are not their vassals," they protested. "Since they are making unilateral decisions, we will secede from the federation."

The annual burden of paying Kosovo's health, education, and welfare costs, as well as supporting the army stationed there, was about $1.5 billion by 1991, and I believe it has remained at that level or grown even larger. But after 1991, it was Serbia's burden to carry alone.

When I met Milosevic in 1991, I asked him how Serbia could afford to continue paying Kosovo's bills, and also how he planned to regain Kosovo for the Serbs. "Two million people are not fog that will have disappeared when you wake up one morning," I warned him. "Where will they go? You cannot force them into Macedonia. It would scare the daylights out of Greece, which has Muslims on its southern border, in Turkey, and won't tolerate having the Kosovo Muslims on its northern border." (I was well aware of this fear, because I was also consulting for the Greek government at that time.)

> I told Milosevic, "Two million people are not fog that will have disappeared when you wake up one morning."

"NATO will intervene," I continued. "Nor can you push them into Albania, one of the poorest countries on earth, or into Italy.

"The Albanian population is in Kosovo to stay. That is the reality, and there is no escape from it. They do not want to be part of Serbia, and it is costing you a fortune to support them, while meanwhile they are multiplying.

"Furthermore, how long can you sit on bayonets, anyway?" I asked, rephrasing a quip attributed to Talleyrand.[2]

---

[2] Charles Maurice de Talleyrand-Périgord, Napoleon's foreign minister, famously said, "You can do anything with bayonets except sit on them."

"You have to let go of Kosovo," I insisted. "How you got to power is not how you are going to stay in power." Kosovo, I told Milosevic, was "the Serb gangrene," because the problem kept spreading.

A Reality Check

"How many Albanians are now in Belgrade?" I asked.

"About forty thousand," was the answer.

"That is how many there were in Kosovo forty years ago," I said. "And now there are two million. So forty years from now, Albanians will be the majority in Belgrade, too. And you, the Serbs, will be a minority in your own country.

"That is what happened to the Afrikaans in South Africa, and what *will* happen to the Jews in Israel, unless there is major Jewish immigration to Israel from abroad. If the Jewish immigration from the Soviet Union had not occurred, Arabs would be the majority in Israel already.

"Cut your losses. Walk away from Kosovo, or over time it will endanger all of Serbia," I warned him, and I repeated that warning to each subsequent Serbian government.

But symbols are more powerful than reasoning. And emotions are stronger than logic.

As we all know, Milosevic chose ethnic cleansing as his strategy for regaining control of Kosovo. In response, NATO attacked Serbia and kicked the Serbs out of Kosovo. Now Kosovo has declared independence. But in reality, Serbia had lost its Jerusalem, its Mecca, long before that declaration of independence.

Why couldn't Milosevic or subsequent governments give up Kosovo and cut their losses?

Despite the repercussions that holding onto Kosovo entailed, no Serbian politician could politically afford to let go. Imagine that an Israeli leader tried to hand over jurisdiction of the Western Wall to the Arabs. Is there any Israeli politician who could survive politically in the aftermath? What about a Muslim leader who agreed to let Mecca become independent? That would be the abrupt end of his career, right?

All Serbian politicians worry about what history will say of them. They know that whoever gives Kosovo away will forever be known as Serbia's

Judas, the traitor who sold the motherland. And most people will believe there was a heavy bribe involved, because no other explanation will make sense to them.

Furthermore, the leader who gives up Kosovo will immediately be thrown out of office and into prison, because such an act actually violates the Serb constitution.

So Serbia was stuck. It spent billions of dollars to hold onto Kosovo, then it lost Kosovo anyway, first to NATO and then to United Nations forces. It cannot get Kosovo back free of Albanians, nor can it rule Kosovo by force. Kosovo's independence is a done deal.

But note the irony: Kosovo's independence is the best thing that could have happened to Serbia. What Serbian politicians could not do themselves was done for them. The gangrenous limb Serbia could not bring itself to amputate is finally gone. Now, Serbia is free to devote its energies and resources to *Serbia*, not to a province whose population hates Serbia and would never have given it a return on its investment.

But, because Kosovo is a symbol, the opera is not over yet. The fat lady has not sung. I cannot say when, but I predict that if Kosovo and Serbia do not become part of the European Union, thus becoming virtually joined again, there will be bloodshed. The Serbs will certainly continue trying to retake Kosovo. They will not succeed, but until they understand that, the blood will continue to flow.

The Serbs will never forget Kosovo; it is in their poetry, their songs, and their blood. The Albanians will not give it up, either. They will fight back, because Kosovo is now their motherland.

Stay tuned.

THE SAD LEGACY
OF CROATIA'S CIVIL WAR[1]

THIS year I lectured at Strossmayer University in Osijek, Croatia. Osijek is a few miles from Vukovar, a city best known for the massacre of its Croats during the civil war in 1991—a war that resulted in the splitting off of Serbia and Croatia and the dissolving of the Yugoslav federation.

Osijek was not conquered by the Serbs like Vukovar was, but it was surrounded and cut off from the rest of Croatia during the war. Of Osijek's 100,000 inhabitants, only 10,000 remained in the city. The rest escaped to live with family or friends. Out of the 10,000 who stayed, about 1,500 were killed by the shelling. Driving around, I could still see many buildings with bullet holes and shrapnel damage.

During the period of the Yugoslav federation, the city was a big industrial, cultural, and educational center of Croatia. Most of its inhabitants were of mixed Serbian and Croatian origin; you could only determine which was which by asking someone's religion: Serbs are Slavic Orthodox, while the Croats are Catholic.

When the war started, they tell me, it was hard to know who was on whose side, because so many families were of mixed nationalities. But families broke apart. Parents denounced their children's husbands and wives. They denounced their own grandchildren. The depth of the hatred was unbelievable.

How did this happen? How could people become so full of hatred toward even their own families?

Was it because of religion? It couldn't be, because most of these people were not very religious.

Was it because of language? It could not be, because the Croatian language

---

[1] Adizes Insights, March 2009.

and the Serbian language are very close, like British and American English—just some different spellings and a different accent.

Was the fighting over land or resources? The Croats claimed that during the period of the Yugoslav federation, the Serbs dominated them, taking the Croats' tax money to Belgrade and returning nothing. But that alone would not cause so much hatred.

So what was it? Where did this deep hatred come from?

It must have been nationalism: people's identity, their source of pride. Still, it is hard to believe that this alone could explain the atrocities of that war, when people were shooting each other indiscriminately, killing just for the sake of killing.

My host in Osijek told me that during the war she would listen to a Croatian TV news broadcast, then switch immediately to a Serbian TV news broadcast, trying to determine the truth by comparing the two reports.

Years ago, my very good friend, a Croatian sociologist, gave me an explanation—although he did not dare to publish it—that the people of Osijek confirmed for me on this visit.

He said nationalist politicians on both sides deliberately told lies about atrocities that never happened, in order to get people stirred up and emotional about their national identity. Why? The Croatians wanted to encourage the movement to establish a separate nation, while the Serbs wanted to fuel the resolve to punish the Croatians for wanting to secede.

For example, Croatian TV would report that Croats in a remote village had been murdered and burned, their houses ransacked by Serbs. All over Croatia, the Croats, their blood boiling, would demand revenge. But if you actually went to that remote village, the people there had no knowledge of these "atrocities."

And on the other side, Serbian TV would do the same thing, justifying the Serbs' atrocities and the irrational hatred they have felt for the Croats for generations.

My host in Osijek told me that during the war she would listen to a Croatian TV news broadcast, then switch immediately to a Serbian TV news broadcast, trying to determine the truth by comparing the two reports.

But with such intensity of propaganda and the passion for revenge rising to uncontrollable levels, eventually the atrocities didn't have to be fabricated anymore. They became real. On both sides.

FARMING IS IMPOSSIBLE

The war has left its mark. Slavonia, the region of which Osijek is the capital, used to be the breadbasket of Croatia. It has arable land, very productive soil, and flat, easy-to-farm terrain. But now the land is desolate. Slavonia is one of the most intensely land-mined regions in the world. As one drives from Osijek to Vukovar, all along both sides of the road there are signs reading: "Beware of mines."

Because the Croatian government has no resources to remove the mines, the land cannot be farmed. And as the agricultural industry has died, the purchasing power of the population has decreased, and commerce is suffering. That in turn means Osijek's industry has fewer outlets in which to sell, not to mention that Croatia is a much smaller market than the whole Yugoslav federation once was.

The result? Osijek has 25 percent unemployment. Vukovar has 50 percent unemployment. And many of the unemployed are university graduates.

Croatia is a developed country. People are expected to go to college and graduate with a university degree. But there are no jobs. To emigrate is not easy, but some do succeed in moving to Germany, Sweden, or Switzerland. The best minds are leaving the country.

The older people, who remember how it was in Yugoslavia, claim life was better then. True, it was a Communist state, they say, but still there was work. There was safety. Families were not split apart because grown children moved abroad.

Croatia's young people disagree. Why? Because they have been taught in school that Yugoslavia was a prison state, that the Serbs were plundering the resources of Croatia, etc., etc., etc. All nationalistic propaganda.

THE HATRED CONTINUES

In Croatia, you are not supposed to sing Serbian songs. Croats even developed a language of their own in order not to speak Serbian. The language used to be called Serbo-Croatian. It was one language. Then Croat nationalists dug up old Croatian words used in the Middle Ages, created new words, taught them in schools, and forced newspapers and other media to use them.

Years ago, I could communicate with Croats without any effort. Now I cannot even read the newspaper easily.

Before my lecture, my hosts spent hours debating how to announce what language I would be speaking in. I did not know the new Croat language, but they did not dare to say the lecture would be in Serbian. Nor could they say I would speak in Serbo-Croatian, because that would imply that the two are the same language—and that would go beyond politically incorrect, all the way to politically dangerous.

> In Greece…I dared to order a Turkish coffee. They almost threw me out of the restaurant

So they came up with a creative solution: It was announced that I would lecture in a combination of Serbian and Croatian.

Of course, in essence all Croats understand the Serbian language. They spoke the same language not so long ago. It is as if the Union had lost the American Civil War and now Texans spoke the Texan language, while people from Boston spoke Bostonian. They would both be speaking English, just with a different accent.

I lectured in Serbian and used, literally, three new Croatian words in order to live up to the claim that I would be using a combination of the two languages.

One of my books has been translated into the new Croatian language. All the other books are available in Serbian. In order not to upset the audience, my office staff did not bring the Serbian-language books to sell at my seminar, even though all the participants would have understood it perfectly.

In a restaurant, when I ordered a Serb salad—which is lots of chopped tomatoes, cucumbers, olives, and onions—the waiter was clearly shaken. I realized my mistake, quickly ordered a Greek salad, and told him to hold the cheese. Obviously it was, de facto, a Serb salad.

This reminded me of another politically incorrect request I once made in Greece: I dared to order a Turkish coffee. They almost threw me out of the restaurant. It is a Greek coffee, they insisted. So in Turkey, I ordered a Greek coffee and got a very quizzical look from the waiter. What kind of coffee, I wondered, should I order in Croatia? To be safe, I ordered a domestic coffee.

> Slavonia is one of the most intensely land-mined regions in the world.

I was told that the European Union is making money available to "Western Balkan" states for management education. "What are the Western Balkans?" I asked, and was told: Croatia, Macedonia, Serbia, even Bulgaria. But look at a map! "If Bulgaria is in the Western Balkans," I said, "then what are the *Eastern* Balkans?"

"There are no Eastern Balkans," they said. "They are all Western Balkans."

I leave it to you, reader, to make sense of all this.

'MACEDONIA'
BY ANY OTHER NAME[1]

ONE of the best-known businessmen in Macedonia invited me to give a lecture to the business community of Skopje, my birthplace. I had been consulting nearby, in Montenegro, so I offered to do the lecture free of charge if, in exchange, they would organize evenings of folk singing, which I adore.

When I arrived, I already had appointments scheduled with Branko Crvenkovski, Montenegro's president, and Kiro Gligorov, the former president. But I did not know what I was in for. I ended up in the middle of a political typhoon. My visit created enormous noise in the media, and I was attacked and criticized.

Here is the background:

'BAD NEIGHBORHOOD'

Macedonia is a small country with about two million inhabitants. It borders Albania on the west, Greece on the south, Bulgaria on the east, and Kosovo on the north. It could not have found a worse neighborhood.

Between 25 and 40 percent of Macedonia's population are of Albanian origin. They do not feel Macedonian; they identify themselves as Albanians of Macedonian citizenship. Some will not even speak the Macedonian language. This is very similar to the problem Israel has with the Israeli Arabs.

Albania is attractive to the Albanian population of Macedonia, as is Kosovo, which just got its independence. The borders are quite porous. Families live on both sides of the border. TV shows can be seen on both sides of the border, and radio waves do not respect borders, either. The Albanian population in Macedonia sometimes talks about seceding from Macedonia.

---

[1] Excerpted from Adizes Insights, April 2009.

One member of the Macedonian Parliament, who was also a member of the governing coalition of Macedonia, recently made a speech in Tirana suggesting that Macedonia be split up. That is a "noise" that cannot be ignored.

Additionally, Bulgaria has sought to annex Macedonia for centuries. (During World War II, they succeeded, temporarily, when the Germans gave Macedonia to Bulgaria.) Even today, some Bulgarians claim the Macedonian language is nothing more than a dialect of Bulgarian. A member of the Macedonian Parliament recently requested and received a Bulgarian passport, and some Macedonian politicians are very pro-Bulgaria, especially since it is a member of the European Union.

As if those issues were not enough, Macedonia has an even bigger problem with Greece. Northern Greece is populated by Aegean Macedonians—Macedonians who speak Greek. The Greek government has forbidden them from building Macedonian cultural centers, speaking the Macedonian language, or even having Macedonian last names. These prohibitions stem from the Greeks' fear that Aegean Macedonians might try to secede and join their northern brethren. Thus, when the new state of Macedonia was established in 1991, Greece refused to recognize its name, calling it FYROM, or the "Former Yugoslav Republic of Macedonia." They placed an embargo on the new state to try to force it to change its name.

In the early 1990s, when I was consulting to the prime minister of Macedonia, I was also doing some consulting for the Greek government. I tried to act as a bridge between the two, but no chance. The Macedonian government would not change the country's name, even though all they had to do to appease the Greeks was add the word *Nova* to Macedonia to distinguish it from ancient Macedonia, which included parts of Greece.

Why wouldn't the Macedonian government cooperate? Because those in power did not believe the Macedonian people would support the change in the coming elections.

But as long as Macedonia does not change its name, Greece will not support its entrance into NATO or the European Union. This is crucial, for several reasons. The economic incentives are obvious. But more importantly, it would also, in a significant sense, reunite Macedonia's Albanian minority with the nation of Albania, which applied for EU membership in April 2009.

Dueling Claims to Alexander

However, the nationalistic government of Macedonia will not budge on the name. In fact, it has increased its belligerent behavior toward Greece.

For example, the Macedonian government named the airport in Skopje "Alexander Macedon," which seems to imply that Alexander the Great was not Greek, but Macedonian. Also, they found a tribe in Pakistan that claims to be descended from Macedonian soldiers who participated in Alexander the Great's invasion of the area. They are testing the tribe's DNA, hoping to prove that present-day Macedonians are also descendants of Alexander the Great.

All of this only strengthens Greece's resolve to keep Macedonia out of NATO and the EU. The Greeks vehemently claim that the original Macedonians were Greek, including Alexander the Great, and thus the new country of Macedonia has "stolen" its rightful heritage.

I met unofficially with someone in the Greek government last summer to see what was preventing a solution. My conclusion after these conversations was that both governments were acting like a cat that brazenly climbed a tree and now cannot get down.

> As long as Macedonia does not change its name, Greece will not support its entrance into NATO or the EU.

Over the years, Greek politicians have consistently used the issue of their northern neighbor's name to stir people up, make them angry, and get them into the voting booth. And the media have always played along. (The more emotional the issue, the more newspapers are sold.)

The same is also true for Macedonia. The result is that by now, neither government can compromise on the name without losing face. They are stuck. Any suggested solution, either by Greece or Macedonia, will have to be rejected by the other in order to maintain a strong and triumphant image.

Macedonia's leadership is not budging from the name "Macedonia." They believe that, despite the wishes of the Greek-American lobby, the President of the United States will pressure Greece to accept Macedonia as the official name and will not block Macedonia's entrance into NATO or the EU.

During his visit to Bucharest in April 2008, then-President George W. Bush announced his support for inviting Macedonia into NATO. But, lo and behold, Greece vetoed the invitation anyway. This was a blow to the reputation of the United States, but it showed Greece's commitment to the issue.

What happened in Bucharest was a good reality check. The hope that a Greek veto could be overcome evaporated, and some leaders of Macedonia realized that the name would have to change.

The prime minister now wants to put the name change to a referendum. But emotions that have been cynically fanned for fifteen years are not likely to change quickly. A referendum might not pass. And if it does not pass, Macedonia will continue to be out of NATO and the European Union. The cat will continue to sit up in the tree.

MY ROLE AS GUINEA PIG

Now about me.

I was interviewed on TV and by the newspapers. I said more or less what I have said above, and added that I believe it is the Macedonian people's lack of confidence that makes them so reluctant to change the name. If Macedonians were secure in their identity, it would be much easier.

I also said that origins are not as important as behavior. Here is an example: During the Second World War, a Jewish man converted to Catholicism and eventually became the bishop of Paris. True story. Now, was he Jewish or Catholic? I argued that, while origins are interesting in studying what happened and why it happened, a person should be evaluated by how he behaves and what he believes. If he believes Jesus Christ was God's son and behaves like a Catholic, he is a Catholic. Period.

My point was that Macedonians are spending too many resources studying the origin of their people and fighting to keep the name, to the detriment of their quality of life. And in the meantime, the country is becoming Americanized. Young people do not know their national folk dances or songs as well as they know American pop tunes. National cuisine is giving way to Italian restaurants and fast-food outlets.

If the Macedonian culture is being slowly but surely lost, then what does it mean to be Macedonian? It's just a label.

The subject was picked up by newspapers and debated on television: Should Macedonia change its name or not?

In retrospect, I think the government deliberately used me to check the temperature of the population, to see how people feel about the name change.

I do not believe Macedonia can survive for long with a growing Albanian population that does not identify itself as Macedonian. And if Macedonia does not join NATO and the EU, it will soon be in even more serious danger, both economically and politically. The financial crisis we are in right now has only exacerbated problems that were serious to begin with.

Both Montenegro and Macedonia were facing elections when I was there. My recommendation to both was that politicians should stop playing the blame game. Negative campaigns are destroying the country, and the mistrust people feel toward their political leaders because of negative campaigning only serves to enhance the crisis.

In times of crisis, trust is at a premium. The country is disintegrating. One of the few ways to ameliorate a bad situation is to start reinforcing the trust people have in their government and its institutions.

Russia's Willing Martyrs[1]

I N 2008, I lectured to about 300 executives and MBA students in Kiev. Unfortunately, my overhead projector had been placed on a very high stand, so I was forced to write with my hand raised high. Early in the presentation, I accidentally placed a transparency on the projector at the wrong angle, which meant that in order to read what was on the screen, people had to twist their necks almost ninety degrees.

About an hour and a half later, toward the end of my lecture, I finally noticed my mistake. The entire time, no one in the audience had complained, including the dean of the school, who was sitting in the front row. Not one person pointed out to me that it was uncomfortable to read what I was writing. They all accepted their destiny: to suffer.

A short time later, I repeated this "mistake," but this time on purpose, in Moscow, where I gave a master class after accepting my seventh honorary doctorate. Same results: They all twisted their heads but said nothing to correct me. Everyone accepted the situation, no matter how uncomfortable it was.

I asked them: "How can you sit quietly and suffer? Did you not pay to hear me? So why don't you stand up for your rights?"

Then I realized that this must be something Communism had brought into being: Whether it is out of fear, respect, or apathy, people will put up with and tolerate any condition imposed on them by authority.

That also explains why service is atrocious in ex-Communist countries. The market (i.e., consumers, or in this case the audience) believes it has no rights. People accept what they get and are grateful if they get anything at all.

This silent acceptance of suffering does not limit itself to absentminded lecturers who do not pay attention to their equipment.

I just finished consulting for a Russian company in Moscow. To get to

---

[1] Excerpted from Adizes Insights of June 2008 and February 2010.

work, most people drive for two hours *each way*. That is four hours of driving every day. And it is at an average speed of five miles per hour. It took me two and a half hours to cover the approximately eighteen miles from the airport to the hotel.

That is the *normal* traffic; it can get much worse. When Vladimir Putin, or Dmitry Medvedev, or any of the bigwigs travel from home to the office, or back, or anywhere else, traffic stops almost everywhere, to give them a clear road. The traffic jams are horrendous. Traffic stands still for hours.

Who could tolerate that? But in Russia, there is silence, acceptance, a sense of impotence to make any change.

In this cultural milieu, I wondered, how worthwhile is it to teach entrepreneurship?

It seems that a cultural revolution must accompany the political revolution before a true market economy can be established in these countries.

EVERYDAY CORRUPTION

The problem goes far beyond traffic. I was told by people in high positions—high enough for me to believe them—that the corruption in Russia is total and not even clandestine.

It is not the government as a unit that is corrupt. It is that every individual who has the capability to extort payments, does. This is actually worse than an organized mafia, where you pay off one person and you are done. Here, even if a business pays off one official, that official could be replaced by someone else, and then the business will have to pay all over again.

As long as the price of oil stayed high, this expensive corruption was not addressed, because there was enough money for every corrupt official. But what happens as the price of a barrel of oil goes down? Do the corrupt officials reduce their appetites, or do they try even more aggressively to put their hands on assets?

The Russian people know this is happening. They know the country is falling apart. Everyone knows there is a dead, stinking elephant in the middle of the room. They talk about it among themselves, but do nothing about it. No mass hunger strikes. No camping in front of the Parliament. Not even any outraged editorials in newspapers.

Why? Perhaps because for generations, they have been subjected to authoritarian regimes, in society and even in families.

Broken Families

What Communism "accomplished" was not only to cause people, sheep-like, to accept anything that's done to them. I recently read about what Stalin did to the family unit. The Communists believed that monogamy in marriage was a mere bourgeois convention and should be abolished. Open marriage was not an American innovation; Communism made it morally acceptable and even sanctioned it during Stalin's regime.

What did that do? It broke the family apart.

Another way to weaken the family cell was to teach children at school to report to the police if they heard anyone in the family speak against Stalin. Quite a few parents were sent to Siberia because the children did their "duty."

> In Russia, there is silence, acceptance, a sense of impotence to make any change.

The Communists knew exactly what they were doing. If the family unit is broken, and religion is abolished, then to whom do you feel you belong? Clearly, to the state. And Communist propaganda at the time promoted Stalin as father of the nation.

I remember how, when I was growing up in Communist Yugoslavia, I was brainwashed to think that I was, first and foremost, Tito's son.

In the Adizes (PAEI) code,[2] managers with an (A)dministrative style need to control everything, to mold everything so that it is controllable. Any means are acceptable—and I mean immoral as well as moral means. They will use religion, ideology, and loyalty. (A)s reward and punish mercilessly in order to gain absolute control. An (A) considers any means legitimate if the end is complete control, and if the means are not legitimate, they will *make* them legitimate.

---

[2] The (PAEI) code argues that managing an organization well involves having competence in four specific tasks: (P)roducing, (A)dministrating, (E)ntrepreneuring, and (I)ntegrating. For more information on the (PAEI) code, see my book *Management/Mismanagement Styles* (Santa Barbara, CA: Adizes Institute Publications, 2004).

LANGUAGE CUES

It seems to me that this authoritarian culture has manifestations in the Russian language. On this last trip, for example, as I listened to my simultaneous translator, I noticed that in the Russian language, the word for "solution" and the word for "decision" are the same.

How interesting. It implies to me that, for a Russian, every decision is a solution. As if the decision-maker were infallible.

We know from experience that there are bad decisions that do not produce a solution at all. But in the Russian language, and thus Russian culture, a decision *is* the solution, and there is nothing more to talk about.

Another language cue to authoritarianism is the word for "belt"—the belt that connects regions or entities, or the belt that holds up your pants. In Russian, the word for "belt" and the word for "whip" are the same. My interpretation: To keep things together, use a whip.

AN UNNATURAL FIT

Oddly, there is no translation in Russian for the word "efficiency," even though that is (A)'s *raison d'être*, its slogan and badge of honor. So here is one more insight: One would expect Russia's culture to be dominated by the (A) role, because Communism was an overwhelmingly (A) system. Look at the buildings from that era. As I was driven through the city, I could easily pick out which were built during the Communist regime, and when I asked the driver to confirm my opinion I was never wrong. Communist-era buildings are all big and square and heavy and bombastic: glorified (A). (The same is true for the buildings in Berlin from the Nazi era, or in Italy from the Fascist era—and have you seen Brazil's capital, Brasilia, which was designed by a socialist architect?)

But on the other hand, look at how Russians drive. You can tell a lot about the culture of a country by how its citizens drive. Russians, for instance, do not know what a lane is. They all try to find a hole in the traffic that they can exploit to move forward, ahead of someone else.

This is very much like Israeli- or Greek-style driving; it's typical of an (E)ntrepreneur or (P)roducer, and it certainly isn't (A). If you want to see (A) driving, go to England. They know the rules and honor them without being asked or told. It comes naturally to them.

I suggest that the (A) style so conspicuous during the Communist era was not intrinsic to Russian culture. Russians do not stand peacefully in line. They push and shove and try to get ahead of the other people, like Israelis do. Russia's (A) was artificially, ideologically imposed.

The British have (A) as part of their culture. So do the Germans. I suggest that Communism was not culturally a natural fit in Russia. Rather, it was imposed by Stalin, using force and intimidation. He wanted to change the country, but in a totally dictatorial way. He produced change by issuing death warrants. Millions of peasants were murdered or exiled to Siberia to die: change at any cost, with iron controls.

For Stalin's style, Communism was the best-suited system. But he could just as easily have been a Nazi. It was a question of style, not values.

There is much to learn from traveling.

PART 3

CHALLENGES FOR
THE UNITED STATES

·

THE MIGRATION OF JOBS
IS HAPPENING; SHOULD IT?
IS THAT WHAT WE WANT?[1]

FOR quite a while, jobs have been migrating from the United States to developing countries—India, China, and Mexico, for example—and the reality is that because of this migration, there is higher unemployment in the United States. But is this good or bad? And what, if anything, should we do about it? There are several options.

One option is a protectionist policy, which would impose high tariffs on products and services from these countries and eliminate the advantage of exporting jobs. That may improve the short-term economic condition in the United States. But the question remains: *Should* we do it?

We all realize that the world is increasingly becoming a "village," with a global economy. A protectionist policy would stand in the way of the natural progress of investment. But more important, it would do nothing to promote our competitive advantage.

We are all familiar with the Economics 101 principle that strategy should be based on an analysis of competitive advantage: What advantages does one company or country have vis-à-vis other companies or countries? The United States' competitive advantage is definitely not a low-cost labor force; it is that it's a developed country with a high level of sophistication and technology. Thus, its labor costs cannot compete with those in countries such as China, where engineers earn a fraction of what an engineer earns in the United States.

A protectionist policy would negate the premise of exploiting competitive advantages. Let China do what cheap labor does, and let the United States do what the Chinese cannot do competitively.

---

[1] Adizes Insights, April 2004.

Furthermore, protectionism would increase the gap between the world's "haves" and "have-nots." If business does not migrate to developing countries, these countries will have less of an opportunity to join the world economy. Poverty will continue to rule.

A protectionist policy that might make sense economically in the short term might *not* make sense from a long-term political and social point of view, because protectionism will ultimately have tremendous social and political repercussions. Poverty breeds resentment and, eventually, aggression.

BUILDING ECONOMIC STRENGTHS

We need to look at economic policy in the context of *all* its global repercussions, including the social and political. Our economic policy should be developed with an eye toward the future. It should take into account the United States' competitive advantages and capitalize on them.

Let's analyze the problem using the (PAEI) code, which argues that managing well—whether we are talking about a family or a country—involves strength in four specific tasks: (P)roducing, (A)dministrating, (E)ntrepreneuring, and (I)ntegrating.[2]

> Let China do what cheap labor does, and let the United States do what the Chinese cannot do competitively.

Using the (PAEI) code, it's easy to see that the United States' competitive advantage is not in (P), or (P)roducing. Work can be done much more cheaply (which is to say, efficiently) in many other countries. The United States' competitive advantage is in (E), the (E)ntrepreneurial function. (E) is at the center of economic and financial activities, the stock market, the innovation and syndication of businesses, and building the infrastructure of networks that can compete in the world.

The entrepreneurial spirit could and should work with labor wherever it happens to be cheapest and most available. The upside is that this will bring work to those other, less developed countries, and reduce poverty. That is what has happened in India, where American companies have outsourced a lot of "help desk" functions and software programming.

That, however, still leaves the question of what to do with those who

---

[2] For more information on the (PAEI) code, see my book *Management/Mismanagement Styles* (Santa Barbara, CA: Adizes Institute Publications, 2004).

have become unemployed because their jobs have migrated out of the United States. Instead of protectionism, what we need is more effective and efficient education—both training and retraining—that will enable workers to shift away from fields in which the United States has no competitive advantage. We should be training future generations of people to work in jobs that cannot be outsourced to people abroad; fields where we excel and can continue to excel; and areas where we are falling apart, such as criminal justice, social work, and education. The United States lacks teachers, youth leaders, and social workers, and that is where it should put resources, rather than into endeavors that are already so successful that their excesses threaten to destroy our environment.

THE INEVITABLE COSTS

Unfortunately, the older people who work in dying industries are the victims of these tremendous transitions and they do bear the cost. They may not be able to make the change.

When companies switch from one technology to another there is always a cost for retooling; the same is true for a country. A country, too, needs to allocate resources to help with the transition. There will be a cost to the present generation, but if we take that into account and pay up, the next generation will be better prepared.

Let's take Singapore as an example. Singapore wanted to avoid becoming yet another developing country where the economy is based on the cheap, unskilled labor that part of the world has to offer. So the government enforced high taxation on the textile industry and discouraged the emergence of cheap labor industries. Instead, it invested in the best Internet networks money could buy, so that the next generation of Singaporeans would not go into the textile industry, but would study computer science, become computer literate, and find work in the high-tech industry.

Let us not go backwards and try to protect industries that have no competitive advantage.

This should also be the strategy of the United States. Let us not go backwards and try to protect industries that have no competitive advantage in our post-industrial environment. Instead, let us invest in social systems that promote affinities that a post-industrial society needs, and in the industries in which we have a competitive advantage. That will enable us to go forward instead of retarding progress that is necessary and unstoppable anyway.

We need to solve our problems using the competitive advantages of societies from around the world, not just within our own borders. We have to start thinking globally rather than locally.

AN INAUGURAL ADDRESS FOR AMERICA: ADVICE FOR CHANGE IN BUSINESS AND SOCIETY[1]

TODAY, a new government will be sworn into office under our new President, Barack Obama. We all face many social and economic challenges in the upcoming year, and many Americans are eagerly awaiting some promised changes.

People, by and large, want change, as long as it does not thwart their personal interests. But that is exactly what we need to do: change our values and many peoples' interests. What America needs is a paradigm shift in its system of values.

What is the new paradigm that America needs?

In essence, we need to migrate from a values system where "more is better" to one in which "better is more."

Our contemporary culture is dominated by business institutions and business values, which prioritize profits: the more earnings per share, the better; the bigger the company, the better; etc.

Granted, for a single company, more *is* better. But in the aggregate, when the business sub-system single-mindedly behaves that way without regard for the consequences, it destroys the world we live in.

The principle that "more is better" is creating enormous waste. Our standard of living is going up, while our quality of life is going down. Look at the glut of product choices consumers constantly face. As a result, we have too many cars; it takes too much time and gas to drive anywhere; and we consume too many calories, increasing the rate of obesity and diabetes. More

---

[1] Adizes Insights, January 2009.

is not making us happier. I hear more laughter in developing countries in a single day than in a whole year in developed countries.

The financial crisis was caused by this culture of "more is better." Its goals are characterized by endless greed: *more* credit, *more* profits.

How can we change this culture? You change behavior by changing the rewards system. For example, why don't we increase taxes significantly, but give significant tax credits to those who are willing to live modestly—smaller homes, smaller cars—and those who use alternative energy.

Essentially, we should give tax credits to those who change their goals and values, and tax heavily those who want to live lavishly.

Please note: Our system is currently set up to take from those who have, and give to those who do not have. What I am recommending is a paradigm shift: We should take from those who do not want to change, and give to those who are willing to change.

We also need to change the education system to teach the value that "less is more." Increase the salaries of teachers who teach the new paradigm, but not those who don't. Let's subsidize charter schools that teach the new paradigm, and give parents vouchers. Among other advantages, this will create competition in the educational marketplace to encourage better and different education.

Free Speech, Within Limits

I would amend the constitutional definition of free speech, prohibiting violent rap music as well as TV shows that glorify, or uncritically present, drug use, rape, murder, and defying authority.

Yes, that's right, I am talking about censorship. You may argue that we have free will and can choose what to listen to. But have you tried to teach teenagers what to watch or listen to or read, when that stuff is everywhere? You'd have to lock them in the house or make them live under a rock. Sometimes "freedom of speech" is just a fig leaf for those who corrupt our culture for financial gain.

The principle of free speech was conceived at a time when history required it. It needs to be amended now, because our realities have changed significantly.

I realize this is a slippery slope; once we start censoring, where do we stop? But I would rather be approximately right and make some mistakes than be precisely wrong and do nothing while our children and our society are being poisoned by the uncontrolled and unregulated media. Doing nothing, in our current culture, would be the ultimate mistake.

And by the way, we already do censor. Don't we prohibit children from watching certain movies? Pedophilia is banned from any screen; pornographic movies cannot be aired during prime time, etc. So, for those afraid of slippery slopes: We are already slipping.

We will just have to learn how to get up when we make a mistake and start to slide down the slippery slope.

I think prison sentences should be imposed on celebrities who are convicted on drug charges—and we should double or even triple the sentence if they glorified it in public or advertised it in some way. Why? Because our children are heavily influenced by pop culture and look up to these celebrities, some of whom legitimize and spread sick, poisonous values.

> We need a Maynard Keynes for social values now—someone who will legitimize government intervention to promote certain principles.

I would tax commercial, for-profit art, such as Hollywood movies, and subsidize not-for-profit fine art. I recognize that there can be endless debate over what is for-profit and what is not-for-profit art. But there are guidelines, which I cover in my monograph "Managing Performing Arts Organizations,"[2] that define which is which.

I would build free sports centers to train our children and provide them with opportunities to use their energies constructively. Yes, like the Communist countries used to do.

In our culture today, business entrepreneurs are rewarded with obscene amounts of money, while social entrepreneurs—in the arts, in community organizing, etc.—are surviving at best. I would tax Wall Street and use that money to subsidize socially beneficial organizations and their leaders.

I would stop all subsidies and loans to MBA students and programs, and instead subsidize programs that teach leadership of not-for-profit organizations.

---

[2] "Managing Performing Arts Organizations: Founding Principles in the Management of the Arts" (Santa Barbara, CA: Adizes Institute Publications, 2000; print on demand).

I would subsidize filmmaking that portrays the value that "better (quality of life) is more," and tax films that promote the old values, in which more is shown to be better.

I would stop sending financial support (except for directly delivered humanitarian aid for food and medicine) to any country whose government is corrupt.

THREE-DAY WEEKENDS

And here is the most courageous change of them all: I would impose mandatory three-day weekends. One of those days, let's say Sunday, would be a real sabbath, when all commercial outlets would be closed by law. For one day, no shopping. That would create an opportunity for families to get together and get to know their neighbors. If you want to know what that looks like, go to Israel for Yom Kippur. You will see immediately that it is a spiritually necessary experience, and we need it more than once a year.

Some people will argue that these suggestions will impair our economic growth.

Right on.

As we change our goals, we also need to change how we measure success.

It is time to start measuring our success by social indicators: the crime rate, teen pregnancies, the percentage of students graduating from high school, literacy rates, the divorce rate, and other measurements that gauge our quality of life and not just our standard of living.

THE COMMON DENOMINATOR

What is the common denominator in all these changes?

We need values that cherish and glorify life, that nurture the environment in which we live, that support quality of life, and that integrate a diverse society that is subject to disintegration, driven mostly by technological change.

Will the paradigm shift solve the financial crisis? It seems totally unrelated to the financial crash, doesn't it?

Wrong. In my opinion, the financial crash is a manifestation of the endless greed of our values system—a system that is now dysfunctional. The "greed is good" philosophy was helpful when we were building this country, but now we have built it. The system that was needed then is destroying us now.

We need to change, and as our values change, the financial system will change, too.

I can imagine that some readers will be appalled by my suggestions, because government intervention in social values is sacrilegious in a democratic society.

But government intervention in the free market was sacrilegious before 1929. We crossed the Rubicon once before, and Maynard Keynes gave theoretical legitimacy to it. We need a Maynard Keynes for social values now—someone who will legitimize government intervention to promote certain principles. Economic growth was important then. Functioning society is what we need now. As the needs change, so should the tools.

DRUG DEALERS: WASTED TALENT[1]

WHEN I was in high school, I was among the founders of a move-ment called *Noar la Noar*, "Youth to Youth." Our mission was to recruit teenagers from well-to-do homes to work with teenagers who had special needs but no means, such as kids with polio, or kids who lived in crime-riddled neighborhoods. In my case, I worked in a prison for adoles-cent criminals. They were drug dealers, small-time robbers.

Looking back after many years spent studying theories of leadership, it recently occurred to me that many of those criminals had fantastic leader-ship qualities. They were creative, charismatic risk-takers; they knew how to mobilize, how to inspire.

> Prisons punish leadership qualities in those who are incarcerated. Prisons try to mold prisoners to become followers.

In the prison, I worked with kids who challenged me about everything, who broke the mold, who came up with ideas and initiatives and were not afraid to take risks. I was impressed.

I also worked at a summer camp counseling kids from well-to-do families. They were nice kids, who by and large followed instructions, were easy to be with, listened well, and rarely took the initiative.

So what is my point? I'm wondering if leadership is a personality trait that needs to express itself and is difficult to contain. If so, then when a person has no legitimate ways to express his leadership, he will have to find *illegitimate* channels to do so.

Prisons punish leadership qualities in those who are incarcerated. Prisons try to mold prisoners to become followers. But if leadership is an inborn

---

[1] Adizes Insights, July 2009.

trait, it cannot be eliminated. Instead, we should find a way to channel that leadership in a positive way, for legitimate purposes.

The whole idea of a prison as penal colony needs to be re-evaluated. I bet if we could give prisoners a way to express themselves as leaders, in a way that benefits society, and be remunerated for it, we would reduce the percentage of convicts who return to criminal life when they leave prison.

AN ALTERNATIVE
HEALTH CARE PLAN[1]

T HE merits and costs of President Obama's health care plan are currently being debated at length. I have an opinion of my own as to what an appropriate health plan should be.

My insight into how we can, and should, reduce health care costs is based on my diagnosis of why costs are rising and why they will continue rising even after the government plan is established: Those who provide health care are profit-oriented.

THE DIAGNOSIS

If, as a CEO, your measure of success is how well earnings-per-share are performing in your company—and you know the board will fire you if you are not successful by this measure—I suggest that, almost by definition, you will aim to increase profits by any legal means you can.

You, the CEO, will use research costs as an excuse to charge as much as possible for drugs, while doing the least amount of innovation that will still allow you to claim it is a new drug: Change a single molecule, for instance. With one new molecule, it really is not a new drug, but legally it can be patented, thus preventing competitors from forcing down its price.

Doctors are profit-oriented, too. They invest years in training and have staggering student loans to pay back, and for these investments they want a sizable return. In addition, since they tend to rank themselves by income bracket, it should not surprise anyone that they are revenue-oriented and will try to increase their revenues by ordering repeat visits and unnecessary tests for their patients.

Furthermore, to avoid being sued for malpractice, they often overdo

---

[1] Adizes Insights, August 2009.

testing, which eventually causes insurance companies to charge higher premiums in order to cover those costs.

The system almost seems designed to continually push costs upward.

Today, the government, through Medicare, tries to control how much money doctors get paid and what treatments they can provide. But the result is that the best doctors opt out of the government plan; in private practice they can charge as much as they want and be paid directly by those who have the means.

The doctors who continue to work with Medicare are hampered professionally by what the government approves or does not approve. They also get paid much lower rates than their peers in private practice—in return for which they must submit endless paperwork to the government.

Government controls of Medicare costs—an (A) solution, using the (PAEI) code[2]—result in social disintegration and lower-quality medical care for those who rely on the government for their medical needs. Furthermore, these controls do not reduce the rising cost of medical care; the government has been regulating costs for years now, and yet they are still rising.

THE TREATMENT

I have an idea for attacking the problem's cause, not its manifestation.

To start with, I would make medical school free to students, paid for by the government.

Doctors, when they graduate, would be paid like faculty members at universities: They would have a fixed salary. As at universities, salary increases would be decided based on the physicians' service to the profession, quality of professional services, and published research.

> University professors are not profit-oriented. They are there to serve. So it should be with the medical profession.

Patients would continue to pay for office visits, but those payments would go to a governmental agency. That way, doctors could focus on the medi-

---

[2] The (PAEI) code argues that managing an organization well involves having competence in four specific tasks: (P)roducing, (A)dministrating, (E)ntrepreneuring, and (I)ntegrating. If any one of these is missing, or if any is over-represented, the organization will have certain predictable problems. For more information on the (PAEI) code, see my book *Management/Mismanagement Styles* (Santa Barbara, CA: Adizes Institute Publications, 2004).

cal services they are providing, with no financial incentives clouding their judgment. (Naturally, it would be illegal to take payments under the table.)

University professors are not profit-oriented. They are there to serve. So it should be with the medical profession.

All medical research should be financed by the government. Rights to all discoveries and innovations would belong to the government, which could license the production and distribution of drugs to the drug companies. That would cut the cost of drugs. Today, drug companies seek enormous profits, claiming they need them to continue developing new drugs. Under my plan, their profits would be controlled, because the government would determine, as licensors usually do, the price charged for the drugs.

The licensing could be determined by a bidding process: The drug company that wins the license would be the one that bids lowest.

Medical journals would be owned and published by the government, and no advertising would be permitted. Today, drug companies advertise extensively in medical journals and thus have lots of influence over what is published.

Another way drug companies control content is by paying doctors large sums to do the kind of research they prefer. This is a conflict of interest, because these are exactly the kind of financial incentives that can cloud the professional judgment of the researcher.

I suggest that funding research publicly, licensing production and distribution, and putting doctors on salary will cut the costs of health care dramatically.

What is left to discuss is insurance: If insurance companies are profit-oriented, won't the cost of insurance continue to go up and would you not expect that they will cut out anyone who is "too sick" to be covered? Thus, we need a not-for-profit insurance plan that covers everyone.

GET PROFIT MOTIVE OUT OF MEDICINE

Granted, the subject is highly complicated. Far from offering a comprehensive solution, I am trying first to identify the source of the problem, which I believe is the profit motive. If the source of the problem is not dealt with, no solution will work. Bureaucratic controls will merely treat the symptoms and arrest the manifestations. And that is not good enough.

HOLLYWOOD'S DESTRUCTIVE MESSAGE[1]

TRAVELING to Minsk recently brought back memories from my childhood after the Second World War: memories of suffering from the cold, the gusting wind, the freezing snow. In such weather I had no desire to get out and visit anything. So at night I watched lots of television. And an insight came to me.

Before I left home for this trip, American newspapers were criticizing Ms. Karen Hughes, who was President Bush's director for public diplomacy, for failing to project a positive image of the United States. Furthermore, the papers said, no one has ever really succeeded in this job, and the United States has done a terrible job in promoting its image.

Why does America have such a negative image? Is it that the people assigned to promote a good image are incompetent, or is there something else involved? Granted, we are engaged in an unpopular war—but could there be more to it? How was this terrible image created?

As I was surfing the television channels in Minsk, I again saw something I have noticed all over the world: At least 60 percent of what is being broadcast abroad consists of American television series and TV movies, either dubbed or with subtitles, and filled with lots of promiscuous sex, infidelity, and insensitive violence. These programs also project a strong anti-authority, anti-establishment, and anti-parent attitude. Woody Allen once quipped that in Hollywood they do not throw away their trash; they make TV series out of it. I definitely agree with him.

And the world buys those trashy shows. They are cheap. And they appeal especially to people of low socioeconomic status.

But these shows create a serious cultural collision. In Eastern Europe,

---

[1] Excerpted from Adizes Insights, January 2008.

authority is respected. Europeans also broadcast sing-alongs, in which they extol the virtues of their country. They are proud of their heritage, their flag, their national costume. In America, in contrast, we allow people to burn the flag. Our TV series *Married with Children*, which I have seen in at least a dozen countries, is not always understood as a parody. Abroad, it looks like the real thing. And what about *Desperate Housewives* and *Sex and the City*? People abroad think the values they portray are normal and acceptable in America.

The image we project goes beyond TV. Look at our movies. We present our elected leaders as corrupt and/or incompetent, and constantly portray corruption inside the CIA, the FBI, and the White House. We *are* sending the world a specific image of America—from Hollywood, the best machine in the world for projecting images—and it's an image that not only does not endear us to other cultures but must actually scare them. Imagine how people in other countries—especially those where the male is a dominant figure—feel watching *Sex and the City*, for instance.

This gave me another insight: I watch Israeli television, which is broadcast across its borders, and I can only imagine how a Muslim must feel: He sees homosexuals and lesbians starring in lots of shows, women dominating and screaming at their husbands, and children rejecting their parents' authority. To a Muslim's eyes, Israel is not only the country that displaced the Palestinians. It is not only perceived as a base of American military imperialism. It is also seen as a cultural threat to the values of the region. Under these circumstances, how can they possibly welcome it with open arms?

> *Imagine how people in other countries— especially those where the male is a dominant figure—feel watching* Sex and the City, *for instance.*

One more point: When I watch the credits of these TV shows, I see many Jewish names, and I start to wonder when a backlash will occur. When will latent anti-Semitic forces come out into the open and say, "The Jews are ruining our children, our way of life"? I fear that is inevitable.

Accentuate the Positive!

Sometimes, something positive does squeeze through. In my travels, people have told me how impressed they were that Nixon was forced to resign because he lied and violated the Constitution that he'd sworn to defend. That happens only in America, they said. And when Al Gore conceded to Bush in the 2000 presidential election—an election that raised questions about whether the votes had been counted accurately—the people I talked to around the world were moved by how conscientiously and automatically we abided by the decision of the U.S. Supreme Court. In other countries, there would have been riots or even a civil war.

I watched from my hotel in Berlin the YouTube debate among the Republican presidential candidates, and could not imagine such a civilized debate taking place anywhere else in the world. In America, after the debate, the men who had attacked each other actually shook hands. You could not have seen this in Israel or Mexico or Greece or Italy, or anywhere else in the world, for that matter. Americans know how to disagree without being disagreeable. Why don't we promote our *positive* culture—our democratic system? Not just how it works mechanistically, but as a cultural phenomenon?

A cultural war is on, and these TV programs and movies, in my opinion, are causing a lot of damage.

PART 4

CHALLENGES IN
THE FINANCIAL CRISIS

My Take on the Financial Crisis of 2008[1] (Part 1)

LIKE everybody else, I've been listening to the news. What I find as a common denominator is that commentators, analysts, opinion papers, and authors are all looking for culprits: Who is responsible for the breakdown of the financial institutions?

Some accuse the leadership of the financial institutions and their greed. Others accuse the regulatory agencies, which fell asleep on the job. Still others point fingers in the direction of the Federal Reserve Bank, which should have known better, etc.

I think we should care less about who did it and more about how it happened. We need to look at the system that created the mess.

Twenty-five years ago, when I consulted with some of the leading banks, many top executive bankers told me in private, "Honestly, Dr. Adizes, we don't know what is going on anymore." What they meant was that macro-economic theory had not adapted to and absorbed the junk bonds, derivatives, cash equivalents, reverse equity swaps, and God only knows what other financial instruments that had been created.

For instance, some expert economists told me that when tallying how much money was in the market in order to measure flow, the system did not take cash equivalents into account.

In other words, reality outpaced theory. Both the economists and the regulatory agencies were in the dark about what was happening.

So, why did they not say so? Because people expect authorities to understand and to be in control. The "experts" could not admit in public that the emperor was nude.

---

[1] Adizes Insights, October 2008.

Some years ago, I interviewed Michael Milken, the junk-bond king who went to jail. "When did you know you were in trouble?" I asked him.

"Long before I was sentenced," he said. "With billions of junk bonds floating around, the government was getting scared. They did not know what would happen if the bonds defaulted. They had to stop me one way or another, and they did."

In the end, junk bonds did not sink us. Sub-prime mortgages did. But they have one thing in common: The market had changed so much that it simply outpaced the existing system's ability to manage it.

Take banks, for instance. Banks sold mortgages; then they collateralized them and sold them in the market. They sold their risk to the buyers of those securitized mortgages, increasing their profitability. Then the mortgage-based stock got sold again. In the process, risk was transferred further and further away from its source. Buyers then bought insurance against the default of those packaged mortgages, and the insurers got re-insured. Everyone involved was doing his or her own cost-benefit analysis, following the profit goal, and taking supposedly calculated risks.

> Greed—not of any one person, nor of any certain class of people—was stronger than the fear of impeding disaster.

But estimating risk is a subjective decision, and the further the risk migrated from its source, the murkier it got. It became increasingly difficult to understand where the risk really was. Who was holding the bag was not clear. Everyone expected that somebody else was holding the bag, or perhaps they all assumed that the bag would never be opened, meaning that the economy would continue to grow and those loans would never default.

Furthermore, since the mortgages were packaged, it was difficult to evaluate how much those financial instruments were actually worth. How much should they have been valued on the balance sheet? It is not a calculus of $2+2 = 4$. Not even the purchase price truly reflected value: A purchase price actually reflects only the relative power of the negotiating parties. The real, true value can only be known when the mortgages are collected.

As the mortgages started to default, the risk became higher and the value of those instruments became lower, and finally all hell broke loose.

THE WAGES OF GREED

It should not have been a surprise. Years ago, Prof. Charles Kindleberger, the famous MIT economist, warned the world that the housing bubble would burst. Still, greed—not of any one person, nor of any certain class of people—was stronger than the fear of impeding disaster. Everyone—those who took mortgages they could not afford to pay, the banks that securitized and sold them, and the people who bought these stocks—made their cost-benefit analysis and took the risks.

Capitalism encourages greed, even legitimizes it. In America especially, pursuing the profit motive exclusively is totally acceptable, even applauded and rewarded. And *not* pursuing it single-mindedly is penalized. If, for instance, a banker had refused to sell sub-prime mortgages, her bank would have made lower profits than the competition, and she would have been fired for non-performance.

There is a folk expression in the Balkans: "When you join the *kolo* [a circle dance], you have to dance." Everybody was in on the dance of profit-seeking, and they acted accordingly.

But where were the regulatory agencies? Why did they not do something?

Do what? The balance sheets did not reveal the problem, because the value of mortgages, and all these different creative financial instruments, is determined by subjective evaluation, which is not precise. Thus, I suggest to you that the regulatory agencies did not know what was happening. And even if they did, they did not have the tools to put a stop to the impeding collapse.

Who is to blame? Everyone, and thus no one.

Disasters like this have to happen so that we can learn what has changed, and what new system needs to be developed to deal with the new realities.

Stop looking for culprits. Fix the system fast and in an orderly fashion instead.

MY TAKE ON THE
FINANCIAL CRISIS OF 2008[1]
(PART 2)

THE Insight in which I expressed my opinion about the financial crisis[2] generated a bigger response from readers than any of the more than sixty Insights I have written in the last five years. Almost all asked me what I think should be done.

I do not have the solution, and there should not be a single solution anyway. This crisis is complex, to the point that it demands an interactive, organic solution, i.e., continuous monitoring and changing of whatever the solution is. In management parlance, we say we need a "continuous improvement system" rather than a solution we can apply and then forget about.

Why is that?

> Entrepreneurs come and go. Bureaucrats accumulate.

Because the problem is new and systemic; thus, to expect to find one solution that works is unrealistic. Even in medicine, which has been around for many more years than the study of economics, in complex medical problems the doctor continually monitors whether and how you are improving and changes the treatment accordingly—because until you are healthy, the doctor does not know whether the medicine worked or not.

What should this continuous improvement system look like? To explain it, I will be using the tools of the Adizes Methodology, which, because of time and space, cannot be fully explained here. For those readers who cannot follow my alphabet soup, please review the material in my book *Managing*

---

[1] Adizes Insights, October 2008.

[2] "My Take on the Financial Crisis of 2008 (Part 1)," see previous chapter.

Corporate Lifecycles,[3] or at least the chapter on lifecycles in my earlier book *How to Solve the Mismanagement Crisis*.[4]

Let us have a historical perspective first:

The Great Depression gave birth to the New Deal.

Where was the United States on its lifecycle then? Before 1929, the United States was in the roaring, Go-Go stage of its lifecycle, until the uncontrolled market crashed (predictable for a system in Go-Go). The system was in need of strong (A)dministration, or (A).[5]

Maynard Keynes' theory of economics gave us the theoretical foundations that legitimized the role of government and gave it the tools to regulate market forces. The New Deal was born, and the government began to share responsibility with the "hidden hand" of the market forces.

With this new economic theory and practice, the United States was well prepared to cross through the Adolescence stage of the lifecycle and, somewhere around the 1950s, reach Prime.

The country is now, in my judgment, starting its slide into the Aging stage.

What caused it to get to Prime is exactly what is causing it to get *out* of Prime: (A), the role of government. Government's regulatory role needed to be born, but over time it grew to be too big and too involved, which is typical of the (A) role.

In Hebrew, there is an expression: "Friends come and go. Enemies accumulate." Adapting this expression to explain the (A) phenomenon, I would say: "Entrepreneurs come and go. Bureaucrats accumulate."

I suggest that the increase in (A)—the role the government plays, which everyone calls "the bureaucracy in Washington"—is what got the system out

---

[3] *Managing Corporate Lifecycles* (Santa Barbara, CA: Adizes Institute Publications, 2004). This book outlines the predictable stages any organization will experience as it is born, grows, and ages. These include Courtship, Infancy, Go-Go, Adolescence, Prime, and, if the organization cannot maintain itself in Prime, the stages of Aging: Aristocracy, the Witch-Hunt, Bureaucracy, and Death.

[4] *How to Solve the Mismanagement Crisis* (Santa Barbara, CA: Adizes Institute Publications, 1980).

[5] A key part of the Adizes methodology is the (PAEI) code, which argues that managing an organization well involves having competence in four specific tasks: (P)roducing, (A)dministrating, (E)ntrepreneuring, and (I)ntegrating. If any one of these is either missing or over-represented, the organization will have certain predictable problems. For more information on the (PAEI) code, see my book *Management/Mismanagement Styles* (Santa Barbara, CA: Adizes Institute Publications, 2004).

of Go-Go, but it is also what is now causing it to age. The New Deal, which was functional once, eventually became the system of entitlement that is dysfunctional now.

NO CHECKS AND BALANCES

These developing symptoms of Aging explain why both presidential candidates are promoting the idea of "change": It *is* what the system needs.

But what kind of change?

The cause of the breakdown in 1929 is similar to the cause of our current problems. The problem was then, and is now, systemic in nature.

Then, the risk associated with companies' excessive inventory was manageable. Accumulatively throughout the whole system, however, it was a disaster.

We have a different systemic problem now: For individuals who took loans, the risk was a manageable risk, but when mortgages were collateralized and amalgamated in order to be insured, the magnitude of the problem changed.

The common denominator is that in both cases, there were no systemic checks and balances.

The systemic solution of 1929 was to increase (A), giving the government a role to play in economic regulation. But employing the same solution now would be a disaster, because we are not at the same place in the lifecycle.

More of the same—more regulation, more intervention—will not work. Increasing mechanistic regulation—more government intervention—will only accelerate the system's slide down the lifecycle curve toward Aging; we will bureaucratize the system even more. We will suffocate the market.

A government bailout of the banks is not a solution, either. It merely arrests the problem, temporarily keeping it from becoming worse. That is all.

What *is* the solution, then?

To use Paul Watzlawick's conceptual framework, we need a change of orders 2 and 3, not of order 1.[6]

------

[6] For further information on Watzlawick's conceptual framework, see *Change: Principles of Problem Formation and Problem Resolution,* by Paul Watzlawick, John Weakland, and Richard Fisch (New York: W.W. Norton and Co., 1974).

First-order change is to change *what* we do. That means more, or in this case, less, of what the government does. Second-order change is to change not what we do, but *how* we do it: to change the system. Third-order change, which is the deepest and thus the most difficult, is to change *who* we are and *what we stand for*.

In other words, the old model does not work. No use tinkering with it and fixing it anymore. We need a new model, a new conceptual framework—almost a new ideology.

The solution requires entrepreneurial thinking and integration—(E) and (I)—if we are going to avoid the Aging predicament.

An (EI) solution is systemic and organic; it looks at the system and how it operates, how the pieces interrelate.

We need change on the order of the New Deal, a radical departure from where we are now. We need a new Keynes to give us a new economic theory that defines the role of government in the economy.

What we need is not "more" or "less." We need "different." We need to re-engineer how the total system works.

THE PRESIDENTIAL CANDIDATES' STYLES

That brings me to a comparison of the presidential candidates, on one of whose shoulders the responsibility of re-engineering the system will fall.

I have worked with air force fighter pilots. I consulted to the Israeli Air Force and reorganized the premier testing ground for the American Naval Air Force. A good jet fighter has to be (PE) in style: a strong producer and strong entrepreneur. He must think fast. Make choices fast. Be creative and be flexible and shoot first.

That is John McCain. His values are impeccable. His loyalty to this country is admirable. His intentions are honorable and his integrity beyond doubt. And he has experience and a proven record of crossing the aisle to do what is best for the country.

That is all well and good … but he is a fighter pilot. He makes decisions on the run. He is sharp, fast-thinking, impatient, very flexible (thus the maverick image), and quick on the trigger. If he is elected, he will make decisions quickly but often change direction at a whim.

Evidence? Look at how he chose a running mate. Another example: He tried to cancel the first presidential debate because of the financial crisis and flew to Washington, behaving as if he were indispensable to saving the economy; then changed his mind and decided to hold the debate after all—all within a few days. He has replaced his top campaign team more than once, too. Fighter pilots do not make decisions by consultation. They are alone in the cockpit and make their decisions in seconds.

In short, McCain is not a systemic thinker. Expect action, but taking into account the complexity of the system, his style can produce solutions that have collateral damage.

While McCain's style is (PE), I read Barack Obama's style as (EI): a strong entrepreneur as well as a strong integrator.

He is creative, but he seems to listen well. He has good judgment of people: He has not changed his campaign team, and this team has made good decisions all along.

> We need a new model, a new conceptual framework— almost a new ideology.

He does not have experience, true. But a leader can add experience by surrounding himself with the right kind of people, as long as he can listen and make good judgments.

As I have said in many of my lectures, what makes a good leader is not what he *knows* but what he *is*.

The United States is at a point in its lifecycle that calls for a strategic re-engineering of the system. We need another Franklin Roosevelt: someone who is charming, who can raise our hopes and restore our confidence along the way; who can listen and think with others, learn and teach at the same time.

Less action, more thinking is what we need.

I cannot predict whether Obama, if elected, will perceive the depth of the systemic changes needed, or whether he will have the courage and dogged commitment to make these changes. Or whether he will have the strength of character to keep adjusting and improving the system—which means not sticking to any one doctrine and being able to tolerate constant flux.

We need fresh, new, systemic thinking. We need a leader who can do that.

And that is the platform, the prerequisite, for the solution to emerge.

WHAT CAUSED THE CREDIT CRISIS, AND WHAT IS THE SOLUTION?[1]

O N June 17, 2009, President Barack Obama announced sweeping new regulations as an additional remedy to the credit crisis. This was, of course, in addition to the solution of first resort: to flood the market with government money.

Most economists saw the earlier move, extreme as it was, as necessary. Still, experts say it will take about two years for that money to make its way through channels and filter down to consumers, and thus for the market to regain confidence. Until that happens, we may be stuck in the same negative feedback loop we are experiencing right now: If people don't start spending again, demand will be lower, which will lead companies to reduce labor costs, which increases people's fears, which causes them to spend less—and so the cycle repeats itself.

So how long will the recession last? Here is what I believe: The credit crunch, or the financial crisis, is a manifestation of a greater problem and not the problem itself.

Before we can analyze whether the Obama Administration's mountains of cash and new regulations are likely to solve the problem, we must define what the problem *is*.

Is the problem the housing collapse? The stock market collapse? The outrageous amount of debt that everyone—from the largest banks to homeowners to students—is drowning in? Is it unemployment? The sudden tightness of credit? The almost universal failure to save?

Is it the fault of the bankers? The traders? The sub-prime lenders? The

---

[1] Adizes Insights, June 2009.

inordinate pressure on government by corporate lobbies? The government's failure to regulate?

Is it greed? Is it a human inability to foresee even the most obvious potential consequences of one's risky actions?

In my opinion, every one of those culprits is just another manifestation of a much deeper problem. The real cause of the financial crisis is that the classic mixed-market model (free market regulated by government), the capital markets system, and the business model of how companies should be governed are all outdated paradigms that do not work anymore. They do not reflect the realities of the new, complex world we live in.

To put it bluntly, the capitalist system as we know it is in a crisis the likes of which we have not seen since the Great Depression. The system desperately needs re-engineering, as was done in the 1930s.

But we cannot simply repeat the 1930s solution and expect it to work. We do not need more or less government intervention. This isn't a question of more or less. It is a question of how to design a new model that is different.

CAPITALISM'S DEATH THROES?

In my lectures and books, I argue that all problems stem from disintegration, which is caused by change.

In the case of the credit crisis, we should start by asking what changed. What was the nature of the disintegration?

Here is my opinion.

The capitalist system is based on the principle that capital creates value and gives a return to the investor. People who contribute capital do not need to literally work. They invest their capital and let the capital work for them. In exchange for that investment, they get a return.

It makes sense, then, that owners should be able to control the company in which they have invested.

This system worked well in the early stages of capitalism—early, meaning back when the owners were also the managers. The major shift from early to advanced capitalism occurred when ownership became separated from management, through the stock market.

In advanced capitalism, many companies are owned by the public, through shares purchased on the stock market. But these shareholders, who are the owners, do not have de facto control of the company they own, nor do they necessarily know a lot about the company. They buy shares because they believe that the stock will go up, and in chasing the best returns they will move their ownership from one company to another in a heartbeat.

The effect of the stock market was to bifurcate ownership of the company from control of the company.

But what about the board of directors? Is it not supposed to represent the owners? Don't the owners continue to control the company, and thus their investment, through the board?

True, the board was designed to be the link that puts owners in control of their company, by representing shareholders and supervising management. But it does not function that way. It should, but it does not. In reality, most boards are selected by management and presented to the stockholders for a vote. Except during a fight for control of the company, the managers' nominees are routinely approved by shareholders.

Admittedly, my exposure to the issue has been experiential rather than through scientific research; still, I suggest that boards are controlled by management rather than vice versa. Management chooses both the board's agenda and the information to which it is given access.

> *Management has lost both pride and shame as controlling forces.*

How about when the board wants to represent—or even is—the majority owner? Does it control management actions then?

I do not think so. Today, businesses are too complex to be well understood by boards that meet once a month for a day or so. Most external boards hardly know what is happening in the company. In making their decisions, board members rely mostly on what management tells them. Realistically, all the board can do is review the company's financial statements, study the recommendations of top management, and be a sounding board.

WHO CONTROLS DECISION-MAKING?

What the board does care about is what it *can* supposedly control: reviewing the actuals and controlling the budgets and, through them, the earnings per share. In fact, under the existing system, the one interest that unites owners, managers, and board members is seeing to it that the price of the stock goes up. When the stock price goes up, the shareholders are happy because their bet worked out. The boards are happy because they have met the needs of the shareholders, and also because the value of their own compensation, usually given in the form of stock options, has risen. Finally, management is happy, because the board appreciates them instead of putting pressure on them to perform better, and also because their own income increases, through bonuses and in the value of their stock options.

MBA schools, business trade publications, and even academic literature all legitimize this common interest. In fact, it is their common mantra: "The goal of management is to increase stockholders' value, i.e., the capitalization of the company."

But in this system, who controls the decisions a company (i.e., management) makes?

The stockholders don't, nor does the board. So who does? It is the ratio of earnings per share that directs the decision-making. The price of shares has to decline drastically and substantially, to crisis proportions, before a board will act to replace management.

It should come as no surprise that public companies focus on earnings per share as the goal to be maximized by management. And it is not strange—in fact it should have been predicted—that financial institutions, in order to increase their performance, took the risk of giving sub-prime loans (mortgages): The risk of default was in the distant future and in any case was transferred to the buyers of securitized mortgages, while the benefit to the profit-and-loss statement was almost immediate. Any bankers who did not take that risk would have achieved a smaller earnings-per-share result than the competition, and probably would have been pressured or even warned by the board to improve performance—or else.

I suggest, then, that the disintegration caused by change was the bifurcation of ownership from control of the company. This disintegration meant that, since that time, those who make the investment and take the risk, the owners, are no longer the ones who control the decision-making. And workers, who risk losing their jobs if the wrong decisions are made, have no say in the decision-making process, either. But management, which does control the decisions, does not take the risks: With their golden parachutes and severance pay, managers can end up very well off even if they're fired.

Let me repeat, for emphasis, where the disintegration occurred: Those who took the risk had no control over decisions; and those who controlled the decisions took no risk.

WAS GREED THE CULPRIT?

Many analysts blame the crisis on greed. I do not believe greed per se is the real culprit. Greed is a motivating force. It encourages people to work hard.

The problem is *uncontrolled* greed. Because there were no controls, greedy managers took risks but did not have to suffer the consequences. (On the contrary, they gave themselves obscene bonuses even as their companies were going bankrupt.) And owners, who should have controlled the risk, could not, and paid dearly for it.

This was not always the case.

When companies were privately owned and controlled by their manager/owners, the situation was different. The owners were building something for their descendants. The family name was on the door. They took pride in what they did. Companies were much smaller, and owner/managers knew every detail about the company. They also contributed to the local community, whose residents they both employed and served. If a company did well, the recognition and appreciation of the community followed. If it failed, its owner/manager would feel ashamed in front of the community. Firing your workers was like firing your own family. The community was where you earned either respect or scorn.

If the banks were privately owned and managed—if they were managed and thus controlled by their owners, who actually knew the people they were lending to—do you really think the banks would have taken the risks that got us into this crisis? But today, companies are enormous, spread worldwide. Clients are mere statistics in a market research report, and workers are another statistic, represented by labor costs and sales-per-employee indicators.

Management has lost both pride and shame as controlling forces. What has taken their place is an idol to worship in the form of a faceless earnings-per-share formula.

We need to re-engineer the system. Specifically, we need to re-evaluate who controls the large corporations—in reality, not on paper.

Let me say right away that I cannot imagine, nor do I recommend, that we limit the size and the geographical presence of companies, or that companies must be owner-managed. Ridiculous. There is no way back from where we are.

So what, then?

WILL GOVERNMENT INVOLVEMENT HELP?

One answer we see happening is that the government is getting more involved—for instance, by taking equity in companies it is trying to save. And which ones is it trying to save? Those that are so enormous that their failure can bring down the whole economy.

But will these companies be better controlled because the government now owns a piece of them? Do we really believe that government ownership will cause companies to take fewer or wiser risks?

President Obama said clearly that he does not intend to manage the companies now owned by the government. Thus, government will be just like any other absentee owner. It will appoint some board members. But why should we believe that the government can appoint better board members than shareholders?

Furthermore, this solution does not provide the paradigm shift that the system requires. If you accept my analysis of the problem, then you can see that the problem remains the same: We expect the boards, representing absent capital (owners), to do the supervision, even though the crisis is proof that they have been inadequate to that task up to now. Why, then, would we believe that these same boards can prevent the next crisis?

Will there be another crisis? Yes, I believe so. After all, this is not the first crisis: Remember the savings and loan crisis?

Let me repeat: The system is broken, and I do not mean the financial system. I mean the capitalist system. It was not built for governance in the complex world we live in today. Our world is globally interdependent. And if each component in this highly interdependent system seeks the maximization of its own interests, it is hardly strange that the totality can get messed up.

President Obama's solution, as announced today, is more regulation.

But is that a good solution? Did the Sarbanes-Oxley legislation improve accountability and thus the quality of decisions that management makes? Or did it just burden companies with an additional amount of stifling bureaucracy and endless paperwork?

More regulation is just more of the same. Again, there is no paradigm shift apparent in the thinking here.

We do not need more of the same of anything. We need a different solution. We need to re-engineer the system.

WHO SHOULD RUN A COMPANY?

So we are right back to the question: Who should control management?

Who do you think knows best how well a company is run? The government? Some wise old men and women who meet for a few hours once a month? Do new regulations or government appointment of boards, or supervisory councils, solve the problem of bifurcation—that those who take the risk do not make the decisions, and those who make the decisions do not take the risks?

No, they don't.

But that is the essence of the problem!

Now: Who is taking the risk of losing their jobs if the company fails? Who (besides the stockholders) worries most about the company's well-being?

It is the employees. They take the risks. They should be part of the governance of the company.

This is how many professional organizations—such as consulting, legal, and accounting firms—are run. And in the aftermath of this crisis, many unions are now exchanging their benefits packages for a package of ownership in the company. In other words, we are on our way to seeing that happen.

But is it just membership on the board that is needed? Germany has union representatives sit on corporate boards; how well does that work? Actually, not well, if those union representatives are isolated from the workers on the line. If they are professional union leaders, all they really know how to do is negotiate hard for the workers.

INDUSTRIAL DEMOCRACY RECONSIDERED

What we really need is to move away from such adversarial relations and toward cooperative relations. A whole new system of governance should be established from the bottom up, from the shift level to the plant and corporate level.

There is a name for the kind of system I just described: "industrial democracy." Industrial democracy was a fad of the 1960s, and I am well aware of its complexities: I have written two books on the subject.[2] Nevertheless, I think it is time we dust it off and re-examine it.

In industrial democracy, it is the employees who vote for the board members and select their leadership. It is a democracy because the people who are going to be led elect those who will lead them, and thus management is controlled by a board composed of both capital and labor.

Democracy should not be applied only to macro systems. It should start from the ground up.

Communism rejected the role of capital in creating value and gave no representation to capital in company governance. Capitalism, by and large, does the opposite: It gives *labor* no power to govern the company. Capitalism and communism, oddly enough, are mirror images of each other, each one rejecting what the other worships.

One more point: The mechanism of the open market is based on legitimate adversarial relations. That is good for creating competition, which promotes excellence and economic efficiency.

But why bring adversarial relations *into* the company? We should leave the adversarial relations to the market, and restructure internal governance in order to nurture a corporate culture in which management, workers, and capital can be on the same side. The more we integrate, the less disintegration there is, and the better off we will be.

Finally, for a global economy, we need global institutions that represent the globe, not institutions that are an accumulation of individual state interests, like the United Nations. These global institutions should not be focused only on economic issues, as the World Bank and International Monetary Fund are. Economic-social-political sub-systems are interdependent—economic issues impact social issues, which impact political issues, etc.—and are becoming increasingly so. You cannot deal with a single sub-system and expect to solve a systemic problem. Systemic problems require

---

[2] *Industrial Democracy, Yugoslav Style: The Effect of Decentralization on Organizational Behavior* (New York: Free Press, 1971); and *Self Management: New Dimensions to Democracy*, edited by Ichak Adizes and Elisabeth Mann Borgese (Santa Barbara, CA: ABC-Clio Inc., 1975).

systemic solutions. We need global institutions to oversee global issues, for the sake of the globe. We need a new Bretton Woods system that looks beyond economics.

Right now, all we are doing is dealing with manifestations, not with the underlying cause. But I am not optimistic that we will make this or any other strategic paradigm shift. Even the current credit crisis is probably not terrible enough to spur the drastic changes the system needs. To really change our financial system, we need to change our values system and our political philosophy, and slay some sacred cows. But to accomplish so fundamental a change, it appears we will need an even bigger crisis.

And that's exactly what we're going to get. I predict that the next crisis is going to be even worse than this one—*much* worse.

We have had the savings and loan crisis, followed by the real estate crisis; now we have the credit market crisis with all its ramifications. Each crisis is worse and more all-encompassing than the one before it, and will continue to be so, until we get the courage to change the values system that has been driving our decisions so far.

PART 5

CHALLENGES FOR
THE JEWISH STATE

THE ISRAEL–PALESTINE CONFLICT SEEN THROUGH A BUSINESS LENS[1]

I N Israel, life goes on. Restaurants are full. Meetings take place as scheduled. In front of my Tel Aviv hotel, people swim in the Mediterranean Sea and sunbathe on the beach—in the same spot where, in 1990, a terrorist's bomb exploded, killing Marnie Kimelman, a young Canadian tourist; and only yards away from where on April 30, 2003, a suicide terrorist set off a bomb at a pub called Mike's Place, killing four and injuring nearly sixty more. About twenty meters away from my hotel is the Dolphinarium, the seaside disco where another suicide terrorist killed twenty-two people and injured about 120, most of them teenagers, in June 2001.

I expected to find the country in a state of paralysis or near paralysis: no one on the streets, the malls empty. But I was wrong. It's true that people are cautious—they avoid using public transportation if they have a choice, and they stay clear of buses on the streets. They try not to congregate unnecessarily. Still, life goes on. More than a thousand people attended one of my lectures; and 350 came to another. Nor were the security precautions particularly rigorous: The guards simply checked your bag and let you in; nothing more than that.

This response surprised me, until I remembered a story (perhaps apocryphal) that I once heard about Golda Meir, one of Israel's first prime ministers. Meir and two religious leaders—a Christian and a Muslim—were asked what they would do if another Flood came and buried the whole earth under water. The Christian said he would pray all day long for God's forgiveness. The Muslim said he would call out to the prophet Muhammad for help. And what did Meir say? "We would learn to live under water."

---

[1] Adizes Insights, November 2003.

JEWISH INDESTRUCTIBILITY

The Jewish people have survived under adverse conditions for more than 2,500 years. They are experienced at it, and they are indestructible. For Israelis, what is happening in Israel now is painful and tragic, but they are getting used to it. Somehow, they have learned to survive under conditions that other nations could not tolerate for long. Very few Israelis, if any, are leaving because of the Intifada. If they leave, it is because the political situation has caused an economic slowdown and they cannot earn enough money to feed their families.

This endurance of, or resignation about, their fate is dramatically in contrast to the reaction of the other side. You can see for yourself on television how enraged the Palestinians become when there is an Israeli bombing of the West Bank or Gaza. But when a suicide terrorist commits another murderous atrocity, watch how the Israelis behave. Do you see outrage? Do you see many people screaming for revenge?

No matter how many are made to suffer or die—whether it is at the hands of Haman, in the Purim story of the Old Testament; the Spanish Inquisition; Hitler; or now Hamas—the Jews learn to cope with it one way or another. Hamas' strategy—to make life so miserable for the Israelis that they will give up and return the "occupied" territories—is bound to fail because it challenges the Jews not at their most vulnerable point, but at their strongest. Jewish history and culture have taught and reinforced the lesson that we will survive as long as we learn to tolerate the pain, whatever form it may take. The various onslaughts are temporary; Jewish life is forever. Thus, the Palestinians will never achieve their goals through the Intifada; all they will achieve is more bloodshed. No amount of suicide terrorism will force the Israelis to kneel down. The Palestinians cannot succeed where even Hitler failed.

APPLYING A MARKETING STRATEGY

In business, a marketing strategy is based on our analysis of our clients' needs and how we might satisfy those needs. A war can be evaluated using those same tools. What does the enemy need? What are the strengths and weaknesses of its culture? What will cause it to surrender?

If the Palestinian leadership could analyze their Israeli opponents using the business model, they would see that historically, the Jewish people become stronger and more united when they are threatened. But just as obvious is the fact that Jews are driven by a strong sense of guilt and a near obsession with justice. Jewish people have traditionally been leaders in humanitarian movements all over the world.

Thus, a very different strategy presents itself: Spark the Israelis' awareness of injustice, activate that guilt, and change will happen.

What would happen if a million Palestinians went on a hunger strike on the streets of the refugee camps, in front of those miserable shacks amid the open sewers, while TV cameras recorded their urgent pleas for justice? Instead of the routine cycle of violence and bloodshed, the real story would come into focus: the misery, hunger, poverty, homelessness, hopelessness, and squalor of an entire people.

The Jewish soul could not endure this sight for long. Very soon a majority of Israelis would be calling for a change in their political leadership and offering sincere and realistic alternatives to resolve the Palestinians' plight. Popular sentiment would turn against the settlements on the West Bank. I am willing to bet that many Israelis would even organize a general strike, if necessary, to force

> *For Israelis, what is happening in Israel now is painful and tragic, but they are getting used to it.*

the disbanding of those settlements, which render virtually impossible the creation of a Palestinian nation with rational borders.

The Palestinians' strategy was misguided from the start. If they had been able to truly see their adversaries and evaluate their strengths, their weaknesses, and their needs, they would have understood that the Jews cannot be destroyed by being terrorized and persecuted. They have become virtually immune to that. Instead of attacking the Israelis physically, they would target the Jewish soul, the Jewish need for truth and justice, and watch how fast change happens.

WHAT DO THE PALESTINIANS NEED?

And the reverse is also true. To successfully communicate and compromise with the Palestinian people, what should the Israelis be focusing on?

Like all agricultural societies, the Palestinians are emotionally attached to their land. Essentially, the Palestinians' sense of security, identity, and pride are as embedded in that soil as their crops and the vegetation their animals graze on. Israel must buy that land one way or another. It must give the Palestinians an alternative for the land they lost, or there will never be peace in the Middle East.

Let us stop looking for who is right and who is wrong. It's no longer relevant why or how the Palestinians lost their land. Let us look for what will work, for a change.

Here is my suggestion: Israel should first accept and acknowledge the principle that it is willing to pay for the land it "occupied," or "liberated," or "settled." Something must be offered to replace the land that was lost. Israel could put several billion dollars into an escrow account for Palestinians who once owned property in what is now Israel, and make those funds available for the building of another home, or buying land, or opening a business. In determining the amount of the payment, a generous sum should be allocated for the years in which the former owners were forced to be without their land and the fruits of their land. Precautions must be taken that none of this money will end up being used to buy weapons with which to attack Israel.

This can be done without admitting any guilt or responsibility for the plight of the Palestinians. It should be an offer signifying good will.

If the Palestinians' standard of living is not brought closer to Israel's standards, then Israel's own quality of life must eventually decline to the current level of the Palestinians.

REMOVING ARAFAT

Many Israelis are now arguing that Yasser Arafat should be expelled from the region.[2] In their view, it is Arafat who is responsible for the inability of Prime Minister Mahmoud Abbas (also known as Abu Mazen) to rein in Hamas and other terrorist organizations and to use his office effectively.

Currently, both the Israeli and United States governments refuse to deal with Arafat: In a speech in June 2002, President George W. Bush said, "Peace requires a new and different Palestinian leadership … not compromised by terror."

---

[2] Yasser Arafat died, at 75, on November 11, 2004.

But the wisdom of this policy is contradicted by the Adizes concept of CAPI (coalesced authority, power, and influence). It does not make sense.

Arafat is there to stay. For good or for bad, he was legitimately elected, and therefore he must be dealt with. Period. You deal with the people you *have* to deal with, not those you *like* to deal with.

How would the Israelis react if Palestinian leaders refused to talk to "the murderer Sharon" and were willing only to negotiate with Yossi Sarid? The Israelis would consider it an insult. Or, closer to home, how would we have liked it if, during the Cold War, the Russians had announced that they refused to talk to the elected President of the United States and would only talk to, say, George McGovern?

We would have been outraged, wouldn't we? "How dare they dictate or deny our democratic process?" we would have demanded.

Let us not forget that it was the United States that insisted on democratic elections in the Palestinian territories. The result was that Arafat was elected president of the Palestinian Authority. How can we now refuse to deal with him? In essence, by refusing to negotiate with him, we are demonstrating that although we believe in democratic principles for ourselves, we feel free to reject a democratically elected leader in other nations.

It is obvious that among the Palestinians, Arafat has the power. And it should be just as obvious that you cannot solve any serious problem by keeping the power out of the discussions. (And by the way, killing him would not reduce his power; on the contrary, it would transform him from a leader into a martyr, thus solidifying and institutionalizing his power forever.)

So, I believe it is time to acknowledge that we must deal with him, whether we like it or not.

An 'Endangered Species'[1]

IN the United States, watching the war in Lebanon on CNN, I seriously feared for the safety of Israel. I have written about this before: What chance does Israel have, surrounded by millions of Arabs and many more millions of Muslims whose rejection of Israel is not a secret and whose hate for the Jews is a formal policy? The Arabs can afford to lose many wars; Israel cannot lose even one, because that one would be its last.

I worry that one of these days, those suicide terrorists will be carrying not dynamite but a tactical nuclear device, with which they could kill more in one day than they could previously kill and maim in a year.

> Why protect the whales and not the Jews? Are they not an asset to humanity? Look at their contributions to all fields of knowledge.

What countries support Israel besides the United States? And what will happen if supporting Israel becomes a political liability for the President of the United States? Can Israel survive surrounded by hate and without global support?

That Israel should survive, and why, I have discussed in previous Insights: The Jewish people, who have been killed and gassed and burned alive for thousands of years, need a safe house. You might even say they are an endangered species. Why protect the whales and not the Jews? Are they not an asset to humanity? Look at their contributions to all fields of knowledge.

But is Israel safe for the Jews, or does it provide a false sense of security that in reality adds up to six million Jews grouped together like sitting ducks, an easy target for the nuclear holocaust that the president of Iran has promised to make happen?

While visiting Israel this month on a lecture tour, I received some insights that I would like to share with you.

---

[1] Excerpted from Adizes Insights, September 2006.

ADAPTING TO WAR—AGAIN

The capability of the Jewish people to adapt, even to the worst conditions, has been validated once again during the war in Lebanon. When the Katyusha rockets began falling at the beginning of the war, the bombarded Jewish population ran for cover, but within a week they had learned to live with the rockets and sirens. Life almost returned to normal. People moved their work to the shelters, and office work continued. In Tel Aviv, which was not in range of the missiles (but not too far away, either—sixty miles, at most) people went through their daily routines as if there were no war. The restaurants were full, and nightlife went on.

I remember sitting in a cab some years ago, on my way to a shopping mall to buy a shirt. The radio announced a suicide explosion that took some lives, about ten miles from where we were. The driver calmly continued driving, and the mall, when I arrived there, was filled with people continuing to shop as if nothing had happened. When I asked the driver how he felt, he said, "What can you do? That is life."

During the Lebanon war, I was watching an Israeli TV channel dedicated to community singing. The opening song, which also closed the program, was "*Lo nafsik lashir davka.*" ("We will not stop singing, no matter what.")

The word *davka* has no translation in English, although Turkish has something similar—*inat*—and so does Serbian—*naprkost*. It means being stubborn beyond logic; to continue to stand your ground just to prove you *can*, regardless of logic. So people sang throughout the program, even though the news continued to broadcast war updates.

In every generation, it seems, someone tries—and tries *hard*—to destroy the Jews. But Jews will do whatever it takes for life to go on. During thousands of years of living under the risk of annihilation, the Jewish people have learned to live their lives despite the continual threats, as if such an existence were normal. They survive. If even one Jew survives, the Jewish people survive.

Moreover, in response to these efforts to destroy them, have you seen Israelis tearing their hair, screaming, and marching through the streets with flags and calling for revenge, as the Arabs do after a bombing? No. You have seen them on television or in newspaper photos crying quietly, sobbing in the cemetery for their loved ones—and it stops there. Life goes on.

Israel is the size of New Jersey. What most people do not know, I think, is that Israel is 63 percent desert. What did the Jews do with this desert? They made it bloom. Go see for yourself: In the former desert, they grow flowers and melons and vegetables and export them to Europe in the middle of the winter, using the morning dew for irrigation.

THE SECRET OF SURVIVAL

I believe the strength of the Jewish people is their ability to adapt to any environment.

How? My insight is that they are able to adapt because they have an enormous ability and thirst to learn. If anything defines the Jewish culture, it is this insatiable thirst for learning.

Jewish people have small families, and they invest in their children. Education, lifetime learning, is a cornerstone of Jewish existence. And where does this thirst for learning come from? From never taking anything for granted. From having an endless curiosity, always wanting to know why. If you analyze any profession, you will find that the Jews end up somewhere at the top. Why? Because they never accept anything as a given, and as they challenge the status quo, they end up leading change.

But, as is true for many phenomena, what is an asset can also be a big liability.

> *If anything defines the Jewish culture, it is this insatiable thirst for learning.*

I can always identify the Jewish people in my lectures. They are the ones who give me most of the trouble. They raise their hands first. They never accept my explanations without challenging them. They are a pain in the butt, and many anti-Semites hate the Jews because of this trait. Jews don't follow the line. They are pushy and critical and demanding.

This trait of searching endlessly for the ultimate truth, for always challenging, makes Israel the most self-critical country I know. Israelis criticize each other to the point of being destructive: In Israel no one is good enough. There is nobody who is above serious criticism and doubt.

Because of that, Israel might destroy itself on its own.

Take the war in Lebanon. On every channel, the television is broadcasting interviews with anyone who is willing to talk, which means just about everybody, because willingness to talk and be heard is not a rare characteristic among Jews. And every Israeli has an opinion about how the war was conducted versus how it should have been conducted. The prime minister is appointing a committee to investigate who is to blame for what they believe was a failure to win the war. (Mind you, Israel did not lose the war; simply not winning it is terrible enough to call for a national investigation.)

In other words, Israel is in the midst of a witch hunt.

This public criticism, which has been blown beyond justifiable proportions, is destroying any trust in leadership: political, military, or even social. Nobody is being spared. No one is exempt from accusations of incompetence. As respect and trust diminish, the willingness of people to fight decreases, and Israel is becoming weaker and weaker.

Furthermore, Israel's apologies for civilian casualties were picked up by the world media. Hezbollah, on the other hand, which deliberately aimed its rockets at civilian targets, did not apologize at all. So to the world, Israel looks like the guilty party, whereas Hezbollah, which started the war and has publicly declared its goal of destroying Israel altogether, is not condemned.

Israeli PR stinks: They wash their laundry extremely diligently and in public, even if the laundry is only mildly soiled.

Belief in Miracles

In Israel, one would expect real estate prices to drop: There is a war, no? There is always the risk that some crazy suicide terrorist will explode a bomb next door. But what is happening? Just the opposite. While the war was going on, the price of real estate was going up, and so was the stock market. The price per square foot of real estate in Tel Aviv is now comparable to the price in Manhattan.

Israel leads the world in patents; it has more worldwide patents than several leading industrial countries put together. It is globally dominant in many industries: Internet security, telephone billing systems, horticulture, drip irrigation, and branded, patented vegetables and fruits, just to mention some. And it has achieved all of this while in a permanent state of war.

Israel is always in danger, but when you are in Israel, you don't feel it. Life goes on. And to tell you the truth, I do not know if this is good or bad. On one hand, it is good, because otherwise how could Israel survive the endless pressure and threat of annihilation? But on the other hand, Israel might be in denial, unwilling or unable to recognize its bleak situation.

David Ben-Gurion, who is considered the founder of the State of Israel, was once asked if he relied on miracles to save the tiny country from disaster. He responded: "We *plan* for them." Today, when you ask any Israeli how the country is going to solve its problems, he answers, "There will be a miracle ..."

WHY ANTI-SEMITISM WILL INCREASE EXPONENTIALLY IN COMING YEARS[1]

IN my lectures, I talk about the importance of solving problems faster than the competition does. To illustrate, I tell a joke about two people who go on a walking safari in Africa. In the distance, they see a lion approaching. One of the walkers—let us call him "J"—immediately changes into his running shoes.

"Why are you putting on your running shoes?" the other man asks. "You can't outrun a lion!"

"I am not trying to outrun the lion," J replies. "I am just trying to outrun you!"

"So, who will succeed?" I ask at this point in my lecture. "Those who adapt to the changing environment faster than the others."

How does this story apply to the Jewish people and anti-Semitism?

BUILT-IN THREAT ANTENNAE

For the past 2,500 years, we, the Jews, have seen many, many killer lions approaching. We have been threatened with gas, fire, beheading, rape, inquisition, expulsion, and loss of our property. If there is a nation with the longest record of being under threat of extinction, it is the Jews.

So in response, we have developed an incredibly accurate built-in antenna to monitor incoming threats or opportunities, and we are faster on our feet than any other ethnic group. We are very intense, aren't we?

We can almost feel incoming changes in our bones, and can identify the

---

[1] Adizes Insights, November 2006.

opportunities or threats ahead of any other ethnic group. And we act faster, because we are always afraid that our survival is at stake.

It is a well-known joke that Jewish mothers want their children to be doctors.

"Why," I asked my own mother, "do you want me to be a doctor?"

"Because you can be a medical doctor anywhere in the world," she answered seriously. In other words, in order to survive, it is best to have a profession that is useful anywhere in the world. Just in case.

Jews have multiple passports. Just in case. Speak many languages. Just in case. Have extended families and friends all over the globe. Just in case. Dedicate themselves to being well educated. Why? Because knowledge will save you when you are forced to move to a new and alien place and must find a way to survive.

THRIVING IN PERIODS OF CHANGE

Because we respond to change faster and better than other ethnic groups, we end up leading change and eventually becoming the leaders in whatever field or industry we enter. Thus, it is not strange that many of the Russian revolutionary Communists were Jews. They led the change. I am just now reading a book about Josep Broz Tito of Yugoslavia, written by Yugoslav historians, and they claim that the brain behind Yugoslav Communism was Mosha Pijade, another Jew.

> *Jews have multiple passports. Just in case. Speak many languages. Just in case. Have extended families and friends all over the globe. Just in case.*

But this phenomenon is not applicable only to Communism. Jews are now the leading capitalists of post-Communist Russia. We lead in all fields in which change requires a response that creates new opportunities for leadership to emerge. In all fields where Jews get involved, they start out as the innovators and end up as the leaders. The more change, the better we do. We were the first in motion pictures: the Warner brothers, Samuel Goldwyn, and Louis B. Mayer were all Jews. We have been leaders in medicine, art, literature, business, economics, and even crime: Meyer Lansky and Bugsy Siegel, Jewish gangsters, were instrumental in founding the city of Las Vegas.

Even if we are prohibited (by quotas, for example) from going into a particular field, when we are eventually allowed in, we are such fierce competitors that we leave the others behind to be chewed by the lion. We identify the changes that need to be made, lead those changes, and end up on top again.

As the changes in this world accelerate, the Jews will prosper more and more, outpacing others who are still wondering what is happening and what to do about it.

But this success has a price. As Machiavelli said, "Nothing is more difficult than to introduce a new order—because the innovator has, for enemies, all those who have done well under the old conditions, and lukewarm defenders in those who *may* do well under the new." In other words, if you want to be hated, try leading change.

How do you think the guy being chewed by the lion feels about J, who escaped? As he lies there bleeding, do you think he applauds J's escape? And if he survives the lion, what is he going to do to J when they meet again?

Because the Jews learned to run faster than anyone else, the world learned to suspect and resent them, even before the lion showed up on the scene.

> In Russia … anyone who is economically successful is called a Jew, no matter what her religion may be.

ENVY LEADS TO HATRED

As changes accelerate, those who are more aware, more flexible and creative, more entrepreneurial, will do well. (In Russia, I discovered, anyone who is economically successful is called a Jew, no matter what her religion may be.) Those who lack these traits will fall into sociological, cultural, or economic traps and end up having less and less. How, then, will they feel about the successful Jews? They will resent those who benefited from the changes and left them behind. More than likely, they will be jealous and seek revenge.

Some simple-minded people will even accuse the Jews of bringing the lion in on purpose, in order to steal the meager resources and let the rest be eaten by the lion: "Jews will create wars on purpose, because they benefit from them."

I believe that as changes accelerate to unprecedented rates, and as the

Jews exploit those changes and succeed, anti-Semitism will also flourish, to previously unknown dimensions.

Change, as we know, can lead to problems or opportunities. Whether those changes are problems or opportunities depends on how fast one can adapt and pro-act. Jews are at their best in dealing with change. That creates jealousy and resentment and can lead to unprecedented tragedies, perhaps even worse than the Holocaust.

CARTER AND THE JEWISH COMMUNITY[1]

DO facts generate a point of view, or is it vice versa?

Years ago, I was up for tenured professorship at UCLA. This was a major event in the life of a young assistant professor: Would they give me a lifetime secured appointment or not?

The staffing committee met to decide. Their vote was seven against me and one in favor.

I asked to meet with the staffing committee to make a presentation. I spoke for half an hour.

They voted again. The new vote was seven in favor and only one against. A total reversal!

Now, please note: During this half hour, I promise you, I did not publish anything new. I did not do any more research. I told them nothing that they did not already know. All I did was change their frame of mind, their "hypothesis."

> It is not necessarily true that people form opinions by looking at the facts first from a neutral, unbiased position.

Scientists start with a hypothesis and then look for data to prove or disprove that hypothesis.

But what, exactly, is a "hypothesis"?

It is a point of view, a theory, a conjecture.

It is not necessarily true that people form opinions by looking at the facts first from a neutral, unbiased position.

I suggest that we often formulate an opinion first and only *then* look for the facts to support our position, or use that opinion to interpret the facts we already have.

---

[1] Adizes Insights, December 2006.

CARTER'S ANTI-ISRAEL RANT

There is a big debate over former President Jimmy Carter's new book, *Palestine: Peace, Not Apartheid.*[2]

What is Carter's point? According to an article in the *New York Times*, Carter is claiming that "pro-Israel lobbyists have stifled debate in the United States over the Israeli-Palestinian conflict; that Israelis are guilty of human rights abuses in Israeli-occupied Palestinian territories; and that the editorial pages of American newspapers rarely present anything but a pro-Israel viewpoint."[3]

Hmm. Ask the Israeli or the American Jewish community whether this is true, and what would they say? Just the opposite: Our PR stinks; the world does not understand us; the media is biased against us. The real abusers of human rights are the suicide terrorists who kill and maim men, women, and children in coffee shops, pizzerias, or on buses. *That* terror is the real abuse.

> The real abusers of human rights are the suicide terrorists who kill and maim men, women, and children.

What Carter calls Israeli human rights abuses are the unfortunate realities of coping with Hamas and potential suicide terrorists who refuse to negotiate a peace settlement, and of dealing with Iran, which openly advocates the destruction of the State of Israel and is probably developing nuclear devices that can make that threat a reality.

Many Israelis and American Jews feel that the media is biased against Israel, that Arab suffering gets pages and pages of news and endless pictures (some of them doctored) while Israeli suffering is hardly mentioned.

Now, whom would you believe: Carter or the Jewish community?

Each side has a point of view that it substantiates with self-selected facts.

This reminds me of a joke:

Moish is sitting in a subway seat reading an anti-Semitic newspaper. Haim, his friend, gets very upset.

---

[2] New York: Simon & Schuster, 2006.

[3] Julie Bosman, "Carter Book Stirs Furor with Its View of Israelis," *New York Times*, December 14, 2004. Five years later, however, in December 2009, Carter wrote an open letter to the Jewish community apologizing for comments in his book that he acknowledged may have "stigmatized" Israel. Almost immediately there was speculation that the apology was motivated by the fact that his grandson, Jason Carter, had entered the Georgia State Senate race two weeks earlier, in a district that has a large Jewish population. Jason Carter is Carter's first grandchild to seek political office.

"How can you, Moish, a Jew, read a Nazi newspaper?"

"Well," says Moish, "when I read Jewish newspapers I get depressed. All I read about is persecution, pogroms, troubles, danger. ... When I read Nazi newspapers, *amehaye* (I feel good): We run the world. We own the media. We control the money. We are powerful."

I believe that Carter formed his opinion first and then looked for facts to support it, instead of deriving his opinion from an objective analysis of those facts.

ISRAEL'S 'TICKING BOMBS'[1]

THE first thing you must realize about this country is that there are two Israels: the one you experience when you are there, and the one you understand only after you've left.

When in Israel, you can't *not* be impressed by the might of the country, by its growth and success: the highways, the high-rises, the hotels. It is extraordinary, and there is no doubt that it is a very advanced and developed country. When visiting Israeli companies, you feel you are at the epicenter of a world power. Elbit, one of my former clients, is now the tenth largest military electronics company in the world. AMDOC, which employs 15,000 people worldwide, is the world's leading company in billing software for cellular telephones, and they are now going into network computing to compete with Oracle.

> As long as the knife is not at their throats, Israelis keep adapting to the deteriorating situation and keep calming each other's fears.

Israel is a success story even without mentioning that it is one of the top Internet development countries in the world, and one of the top countries with a presence in the United States stock markets. Israelis own the Plaza Hotel in New York; they are opening the largest hotels in Las Vegas; they're investing in real estate in Moscow; and on and on and on. Microsoft, Google, Yahoo, and Intel all have their research entities in Israel. Some of the greatest inventions and innovations of Microsoft and Intel were developed in Israel, and Warren Buffet—who, for sure, is not an emotional investor—invested $4 billion in 2006 to gain control of the Israeli metalworking firm Iscar. The shekel is recognized now as one of the world's ten most stable currencies, and Israel's economic growth is among the best in the world.

So how can Israel's existence be in danger?

---

[1] Excerpted from Adizes Insights, June 2008.

That, you suspect only when you are away from Israel. When you are there, the aura of success gives a false sense of security, which evaporates when you leave the country and analyze it from a distance.

There are several "ticking bombs" that threaten Israel—bombs that are not being dismantled.

THE FIRST 'TICKING BOMB'

In our lifetimes, Israel's Arab population will become the country's majority ethnic group. Arabs have a high rate of reproduction, which might decline as their standard of living increases, but probably not enough to nullify the threat. According to statistics I read back when I was a student, the Arabs would already have become a majority were it not for the massive Jewish immigration from the former Soviet Union in the 1980s. This inflow did not discredit the projection; it only postponed the inevitable.

To remain a Jewish state, Israel needs large numbers of Jewish immigrants. That will happen only if there is another spike in worldwide anti-Semitism, or if life in Israel becomes preferable to any other place where Jews can live.

To make Israel preferable to life anywhere else is an uphill battle, while anti-Semitism, of course, already exists and thus is a ready-made engine for massive immigration to Israel.

For the Jews in the Diaspora, anti-Semitism is something to dread. Ironically, for Israelis it actually seems to comprise the best hope for the Jewish state to remain Jewish.

But there is another point to ponder: If massive episodes of anti-Semitism were to drive up Jewish immigration to Israel, the world's Jews would, in effect, be congregated into a new ghetto. This time it would be the size of a country rather than a fraction of a city, but it would be a ghetto nonetheless, under attack not only by its neighbors but also by many other anti-Semitic countries worldwide. Not a pretty prospect.

On the other hand, if a substantial immigration does not occur, Arabs will soon become a significant majority in Israel.[2] They are already expand-

---

[2] In November 2009, I was told that the danger of Israeli Arabs becoming a majority in the country had receded. What happened? New studies have shown that the Arab reproductive rate is actually declining, while the reproductive rate of Orthodox Jews is climbing. As a matter of fact, I am told, in 2009 the populations of Arabs and *haredim*—those religious Jews one sees in black caftans and long

ing into what traditionally were Jewish settlements. Upper Nazareth—which was built by and for Jews because Nazareth itself was Arabic and did not welcome Jews—is now partly inhabited by Arabs, and the Arab section is expanding rapidly. Carmiel, which was established to bring Jewish settlers to the Galilee, is now increasingly populated by Arabs. In Jaffa, part of Tel Aviv, many Arabs refuse to sell their land to Jews, and it is being bought up by Saudi millionaires.

In a democratic country, which Israel is, every citizen has the right to vote. If the Arabs become the majority of voters, can Israel remain a Jewish state? Or could these demographic changes lead to a civil war?

POSSIBLE SOLUTIONS

What can Israel do?

As I see it, there are several choices.

First choice: In order to avoid a potential civil war, Israel could proactively work on changing its culture to become a bi-national country, where Arabs are equal to Jews in every sense. That means changing the flag and the anthem, which are purely Jewish, and designating both Hebrew and Arabic as official languages, which everyone must learn to speak fluently. Model

---

beards—are about equal in Israel today. And since the demographics are working in favor of the Jews, the political "bomb" I described above may be a false alarm.

But this new scenario creates another kind of "bomb." The *haredim* in Israel do not work. They study the Torah. Because they do not work, they do not pay taxes—while consuming the largest portion of Israel's budget for social services. They do not serve in the army, either.

As a result, there is tremendous resentment of the *haredim* by secular Israelis. I have actually heard secular Israelis make anti-Semitic comments about them: They say they hate "the Jews," "the parasites," whom they have to support financially and defend with their bodies in war.

As both the Arab and the *haredim* populations grow, secular Israelis will increasingly become a minority, concentrated geographically along the coast, from Ashkelon to Haifa. Jerusalem will increasingly be populated by religious Jews, while the Galilee will become predominantly Arab, and the Negev, Bedouin (a minority within the Arab minority).

Just imagine what this will do to Israel's sense of security. Secular Jews—a minority in the country, concentrated along the coast—will carry most of the economic and military burden. And serious tension will exist among *three* groups: secular Jews, *haredim*, and Arabs. Where will it lead?

Now, play the next scenario: If there is peace in the Middle East, I predict that secular Jews will ultimately feel more comfortable with the Palestinians than with the extreme religious Jews. Culturally, the two groups are getting closer. Turn on Israeli TV and listen to the music. The most popular music is "Middle Eastern music," which sounds a lot like Arabic music. And a famous Israeli vocalist has already sung Arab music in Hebrew, and people loved it.

I dread the possibility of physical aggression against the *haredim*, whom secular Israelis sometimes call "the Jews." It is already happening; luckily, no one has been killed. Yet.

the country on Switzerland, where people of French, German, and Italian descent live together in peace.

Or Israel might consider doing what F.W. de Clerk did in South Africa: Pass the power peacefully to the Arabs. Then perhaps the Jews will be able to survive within an Arab majority, if you can believe that. (Although how well did it work in Lebanon? Are the Palestinians living in peace with Arab Christians?)

But this solution means that Israel will no longer be a Jewish state. And in Israel, when I raised this possibility, I was told: "Impossible!" Israelis will never abandon the Zionist vision of Israel as a Jewish state. It was established as the homeland of all Jews worldwide; when Jews feel threatened anywhere, they have a home to go to.

Second choice: Insist that Israel is and must remain a Jewish state. In that case, in order to prevent the Arabs from becoming a majority, there should be an exchange of populations: Transfer all the Arabs with their land into the emerging Palestinian state and, in exchange, incorporate the Jewish settlements on the West Bank into Israel.

Except that this exchange of territories is inconceivable. I do not believe the Palestinians would agree to it, because when the fence separating Israel from the Palestinians was being designed and routed, Israeli Arabs made it clear they wanted to remain *inside* Israel proper rather than be transferred to the new Palestinian state. And even if the Palestinians did agree, I believe Israel would not, because exchanging territory would mean giving up the treasured Galilee to the Palestinians.

What about a transfer by force of the Israeli Arabs, away from their land and into exile, thus increasing the number of Palestinian refugees? That would not only be immoral, it would also stir worldwide condemnation, very likely resulting in the imposition of sanctions on Israel and a kind of isolation that would make today's problems look minor.

Third choice: Abandon democracy and adopt a government of apartheid: Take voting rights away from the Arabs, one way or another.

But that would be so repugnant, to so many Israelis, that there would be heavy emigration out of the country, and I do not think I need to elaborate on the international repercussions.

THE NEXT 'TICKING BOMB'

What if there were another Holocaust, but this time a nuclear one? Iran is almost certainly developing nuclear capabilities and has already announced its intention to wipe Israel from the map. True, Israel has threatened a massive retaliation if this comes to pass, and the world knows it has the nuclear capability to do so. A top Israeli civil servant told me that the Israeli government believes the leadership in Tehran is still rational and would not do anything so stupid as to attack Israel and provoke a nuclear retaliation. But who says political leaders are always rational? I believe this is wishful thinking, and I would not bank on it.

So far, I am not aware of a solution to this threat.

THE THIRD 'TICKING BOMB'

Another scenario—not the doomsday scenario of a nuclear holocaust but a disaster nonetheless—is that Hamas and Hezbollah, together with the armies of Arab nations and supported by anti-Semitic countries, might eventually win a war. As I once heard someone say, "Arabs can afford to lose many wars; the Israelis, only one. That one will be their last."

Could it happen?

When you have a disease that requires an antibiotic remedy, the doctor will tell you to take the whole dosage. If you stop too early and fail to kill all the bacteria, those that survive will have built up their tolerance to the medicine, eventually rendering the medication ineffective. The bacteria will become increasingly dangerous and could become fatal.

Israel is not taking the "whole dosage," which would equate to annihilating every last one of its enemies. There is a name for that "remedy": It is called ethnic cleansing, and it cannot and should not be done. But the result is that with each battle or indecisive war, Hamas and Hezbollah grow stronger and stronger, while Israel grows weaker and weaker. The enemy is learning from each battle, while the Israelis are growing increasingly tired of the endless struggle. Israel wants to be a normal country. Israelis have experienced too much death in their lifetimes. There is no family in Israel—not one, I suggest to you—that is not mourning someone who died an unnatural death.

Was the Second World War not enough? Who can tolerate this neverending fighting? Who wants to die anymore? Who wants a war anymore?

Millions of Israelis are calling for "Peace Now!" A large percentage of high school graduates are finding a way to avoid serving in the military. The Israelis are just dead tired of fighting and dying.

Not so the Palestinians. How many Palestinians have you seen or heard demonstrating on the streets demanding peace now, or even tomorrow? If such Palestinians exist, they are at best an endangered, powerless minority of intellectuals. The radicals among them believe that dying for the cause is rewarded in the afterlife. Palestinian mothers actually celebrate the heroic deaths of their sons who "martyr" themselves for Palestine.

In comparison, have you ever seen a Jewish mother celebrating the death of her child? Ever? No. And you never will. Jews sanctify life; Muslim radicals, death.

There is a reversal of attitude going on here: In 1948, Jews were willing to die to have a country. The Palestinians were not. They left the country to avoid the fighting. Now the Palestinians are willing, the Israelis less so. Tell me who is more committed to dying for their cause, and I will tell you who—in the short term, at least—will win.

No Solution to Embrace

So, one way or another, Israel is in deep trouble, in spite of all the positive developments and the country's economic might. Its people know that the situation, as it is, is not sustainable; it does not work. And they also know that there is no solution they can embrace.

So why don't people leave? At least for the sake of their children?

One explanation is that there is a subconscious belief that a miracle will happen. Read the Passover Haggadah: "In every generation they tried to annihilate us and the Lord saved us." Period. In other words, the Lord will find a way to save the Jewish people, just as S/He has done for thousands of years. If you repeat this prayer like a mantra every day, or even every year, eventually you might believe it.

Israelis sometimes attribute the lack of solutions to a lack of leadership and hope that if the right leader comes along he will solve the problem. I believe this is the wrong diagnosis, thus also the wrong solution, because the fact is, there simply is no solution that a majority of democratic Israel will agree to, regardless of who the leader is.[3]

Another reason why there is no massive emigration out of Israel (although there *is* a brain drain—those who have better alternatives do leave) is that life is good in Israel now. There are festivals, music, art, restaurants serving any ethnic food you could wish for.

It is energizing and interesting to live in Israel. So as long as the knife is not at their throats, Israelis keep adapting to the deteriorating situation and keep calming each other's fears. *Al tidag. Yihye beseder*: "Do not worry. Everything will be OK."

And what is happening in the meantime, by default?

Israel might be like the proverbial frog in a pot, whose survival is actually threatened by its great ability to adapt to the water's increasing heat: Eventually the water starts to boil and the frog dies.

Israelis, like the frog, continue to adapt to living with the increasing problems they face.

How can they do that?

One of the characteristics of the Jewish people is that they adapt to anything. This is their biggest asset, to which I attribute their survival in spite of all the disasters that have come their way. They adapted even to Auschwitz. They have survived under any conditions.

Ironically, however, while this is an asset for world Jewry, it is a liability for those in Israel. Israel continues to adapt to the increasingly hot water: Rockets are raining on Shderot, next to the Gaza Strip, and their range is increasing. Now the Palestinians are shelling Ashkelon, and soon maybe they will shell Tel Aviv. They did shell Haifa during the second war with Lebanon. Nevertheless, life in the rest of Israel went on as normal.

One wonders if the frog will ever jump out of the increasingly hot water. Will Israel stay put, adapting and adapting, until it is too late?

---

[3] Actually, I *have* thought of a solution for Israel. It is truly out-of-the-box thinking—*very* out-of-the-box. See the next essay in this section: "Out of the Box: An Idea."

OUT OF THE BOX: AN IDEA[1]

WHEN I wrote my most recent Insights column[2] and said in a foot-note that I had an out-of-the-box idea for creating peace between Israel and the Palestinians, I had just begun to think about my idea. Now that I am putting it in writing, however, the more I write, the more discouraged I become.

As we all know, the Devil is in the details, and in this case he is more awake than usual. So, please, as you read what I have written below, realize that I myself am filled with doubts. In fact, I might be more dubious than anyone else, because I have been thinking about this idea the longest.

Still, bad ideas give birth to good ideas. Maybe someone else, outraged by how bad an idea this is, can come up with a better one.

Let me know if you think of anything.

THE PARAMETERS

Israel wants to remain a Jewish state for the Jewish people. That is the basic Zionist ideology, which I assume will remain alive for at least a little while longer. This means a Jewish flag, a Jewish anthem, the Hebrew language, Jewish education, etc., as well as "the law of return," which grants to anyone Jewish the right to immigrate to Israel and become a citizen.

I assume that the Palestinians want a state of their own, with its own flag, anthem, education, and language.

One of the largest issues is the Israeli Arabs. They already constitute a majority of the population in large regions of Israel, including most of the Galilee Valley. If they keep their Israeli citizenship, they will very soon become the majority population of Israel, putting the Jewish state at risk.

---

[1] Adizes Insights, June 2008.

[2] See previous chapter, "Israel's 'Ticking Bombs,'"

On the one hand, they cannot be moved; and on the other, they populate most of the Galilee Valley, which the Jewish people consider their own and would certainly refuse to relinquish to the Palestinian state.

Nor can the heavily Arab-populated Jaffa, which is an integral part of the city of Tel Aviv, be part of a Palestinian state.

But if the Galilee and Jaffa are to remain part of Israel, the demographic problem cannot be solved.

So the problem, as I see it, is that there are:

- two nations, both of which want their nationality and sovereignty recognized; living in one space;
- intermingled;
- and no one can carve clear boundaries that separate the two.

How can they craft a solution, when the two nations are together by default and yet want to be separate?

THE IDEA (CRAZY AND NAÏVE AS IT MAY BE)[3]

How about one country, but with two separate Parliaments, separate passports, separate police, and separate judiciary systems?

Here are the rules: First, the ownership of land would have to be frozen wherever it is right now. The Jewish people could not buy or expand into Arab land, and vice versa.

No one would be removed from where they are right now. They would stay put, but each nationality would have its own passports, its own local police force, and would vote for its own Parliament.

There would be no borders between these cantons. For instance, Nazareth would be part of Palestine, and Tel Aviv part of Israel. Jerusalem would be the capital of both Israel and Palestine, with a Jewish flag over the Western Wall and a Palestinian flag over the Al Aqsa mosque.

Both Arabs and Jews would have complete freedom of movement, with no visas necessary to move from one canton to the other.

Each country would have its own currency and central bank. Both currencies would be acceptable in both cantons.

---

[3] In May of 2009, I discovered that my idea is not that crazy after all. In fact, it is being considered as a solution for the conflict in Cyprus, where the Greeks and Turk Cypriots must figure out how to live together, too.

To better understand this idea, imagine that many Polish people go to live in Slovakia, and that many Slovaks move to Poland. Both keep their own passports, their own Parliaments and police. The only difference is that they live intermingled.

Also, both Slovakia and Poland—with their own flags, Parliaments, etc.—belong to a larger entity, the European Union.

Something like that might work for the area now comprising Israel and the West Bank.

> One country with two separate Parliaments, passports, police, and judiciary systems.

There must be a body above the two Parliaments to deal with interdependencies, just as the European Union has its administration in Brussels. They would also need a bi-national, common police force—something like the FBI, which outranks state police in the United States law enforcement hierarchy.

This bi-national country, Israel/Palestine, would have one army and one foreign policy. The overlapping institutions would report to the president of the country, and the presidency would alternate: a term for an Israeli chief executive, followed by a term for a Palestinian chief executive.

How would an Israel with open borders deal with terrorism? Like any country would deal with any criminals. Investigate, and prosecute.

My Serious Doubts

This is very out-of-the-box and a very, very crazy idea. I know.

It ignores external forces like Iran, which would take advantage of Israel/Palestine's open borders to more easily support radical Palestinians' efforts to destroy the Jewish state.

It ignores the fact that Hamas and Hezbollah will not agree to any solution short of Israel disappearing from the map. It assumes that Jews and Arabs *can* live together, each in their own territory, without encroaching on the other—an assumption without a lot of evidence in its favor.

It assumes that the Palestinians will give up their demand to return to the land they had in 1948 that is now Israeli land. (Although I do have a solution to offer here, going back to an idea I wrote about some years ago: Israel should recompense the Palestinians for that land, thus giving them the economic means to re-establish their economy. The money could not be used for arms; it could be used only to establish enterprises to be co-owned with U.S., European, or Israeli investors.)

Many problems, obviously, have been left out, because I have no idea how to deal with them. Will the army be only Jewish? If it is mixed, who will be the head? Can a common foreign policy be established and implemented? And on and on, almost ad infinitum.[4]

In fact, I am almost embarrassed to publish this, because the chances of it even being considered are probably nil. But the situation there is so apparently impossible and so complex that maybe a crazy solution is the best way to start a productive discussion.

Again: It is my hope that some of you, outraged by the stupidity of this solution, will come up with something better.

---

[4] A 2009 update: Amiel Unger, in the April 2009 *Jerusalem Report*, made a very convincing argument. He suggested that the real issue driving the Israeli-Palestinian problem is not land or identity, but legitimacy. The radical Palestinians do not want to recognize the legitimacy of the Jewish people residing in their midst. They want Israel to disappear. Period. So no land arrangements, flags, language, or any other agreements will work, short of Israel disappearing from the map. If that is true, the above solution would be worse than just a dream. It would be a nightmare.

ISRAEL AND THE WORLD, BOTH IGNORING REALITY[1]

ISRAEL is facing increasing danger. It is losing its friends rapidly. The worldwide media is particularly hostile. And the Israeli left is helping to feed the fires of animosity toward Israel, charging that Israel violated its own medical/ethical code of behavior during the recent Gaza war.

The fact that rockets out of Gaza are showering Israel and getting closer and closer to Tel Aviv itself, that some of them are hitting schools (luckily, so far, on Saturdays when schools are closed), and that the rocket attacks almost always come at around 8 o'clock in the morning when kids are on their way to school—all this does not get reported.

There is no sympathy from the world media. The daily rocket attacks do not show up on TV in Europe or any other country I have been to. The only reports are about the suffering of Gaza's population. The world's expectations of how Israel should behave and how it should protect itself are never applied to any other country.

Now, I ask all my readers to close their eyes and imagine themselves sitting in their living rooms.

Imagine a location eighteen miles from your living room, and try to visualize it in detail. Then imagine that a country—one that repeatedly threatens to destroy your country—is showering that spot, eighteen miles from your living room, with rockets. Daily, a rocket screeches across the morning sky while your kids walk to school. Approximately 8,000 rockets have fallen without warning from above.

Now ask yourself: After several years of this, what would you do? What would you ask your government to do?

---

[1] Adizes Insights, April 2009.

MINIMAL PUBLIC RELATIONS

Israel is in deep trouble at home and from abroad, and as it loses friends, its time of reckoning creeps closer. Anything could happen.

When you are not actually in the country, you quickly become aware of Israel's dire situation. But oddly, in Israel itself you do not feel the fear or worry. The country is booming. While the world's stock markets were crashing, the Tel Aviv stock market went up.

Israel is busy with its own elections, its own need to keep the economy going, and its worry about the Iranian nuclear threat. Making and keeping friends apparently has a low priority: The national budget has allocated an insignificant $1 million for cultural exchanges and for explaining Israel's position to the world. We all know $1 million cannot achieve much.

> The world's expectations of how Israel should behave and how it should protect itself are never applied to any other country.

Why this aloofness to world opinion? Several reasons, I believe. First, deep inside, Israelis believe that the whole world is anti-Semitic and that nothing Israel does to explain itself will be effective. They have given up explaining.

Second, when you are in Israel itself, you feel secure. The country is thriving: Skyscrapers appear almost overnight, highways are being built, and high-tech companies are dominating world markets. There is a feeling that "we can and will overcome anything."

This sense of invulnerability worries me a lot. That is how the Jewish community of Germany behaved when Hitler first came to power. Historically, this ability to deny reality has come at a price: By the time reality can no longer be denied, the time to do something is long past.

Am I worried about Israel? Yes, more than ever.

IS, WANT, AND *SHOULD* IN THE MIDDLE EAST[1]

LET us analyze the apparently intractable conflict in the Middle East, in which Israel and the Palestinians both lay claim to the same piece of land.

ISRAEL AND PALESTINE: BACKGROUND

Both the Israelis and the Palestinians have valid arguments in support of their position, and each has, at different times, been able to gain world sympathy for its cause.

At the end of World War II, when the horrifying facts of the German effort to exterminate European Jewry became public knowledge, the need for a Jewish homeland was obvious. The Jews' ancient claim to the land now called Israel was also recognized.

Jews had already been immigrating to Palestine in waves since the end of the 19th century. However, that territory had not exactly lain empty since 70 A.D., when the Jews were exiled from their land en masse by Roman conquerors. Along with the remnant of Jews who remained and who could always be found there in small numbers, numerous nomadic Arabs passed through the country regularly in their travels, and many settled there permanently, to farm or graze sheep.

Legally, Palestine belonged to neither group. Having changed hands countless times throughout history, it had most recently been part of the Ottoman Empire. With the empire's demise at the end of World War I, the League of Nations divided the Middle Eastern segment of the former empire into five territorial mandates, with rather arbitrary borders—Syria, Lebanon, Transjordan, Palestine, and Iraq—to be supervised and administered

---

[1] Adizes Insights, July 2009.

by either England or France, with the ultimate goal of becoming self-suf-
ficient, independent nations. France was given the mandate over Syria and
Lebanon, while the British took over Iraq, Transjordan, and Palestine.

Iraq, Syria, Lebanon, and Jordan did eventually become independent
Arab nations (in 1932, 1946, 1941, and 1946, respectively). But after World
War II, the newly formed United Nations, hoping to create a safe haven for
world Jewry, divided Palestine yet again, this time into a Jewish state and an
Arab state.

The Arab nations, however, refused to accept that plan and launched a
war against Israel in 1948, as soon as it declared its independence.

When the smoke cleared, the Israelis controlled a larger area than they
had originally been given, and thousands of Palestinian Arabs, who had fled
their homes or been forced out, were now refugees.

Five more wars since then have only exacerbated the problem—particularly the Six-Day War in 1967, which ended in a rout, with Israel occupying
Jerusalem (previously claimed by Jordan), Egypt's Sinai desert, Syria's Golan
Heights, and the West Bank of the Jordan River, which comprised a large
chunk of what the UN had designated as Arab Palestine in 1947.

The Sinai was returned to Egypt in 1979, after it signed a peace treaty
with Israel, but the rest is still in dispute. In the meantime, Israel has populated the area with settlers, and the conflict is stalemated. The Israelis will
not return the land without a peace treaty they can trust, and in any case
they cannot return everything, because of the settlements. The Palestinians,
on the other hand, will not offer peace unless certain conditions are met that
the Israelis believe will mean the demise of a Jewish state.

The problem seems to have no solution.

IS, WANT, AND SHOULD: *THE SEQUENCE IS CRITICAL*

A good analysis and a solution require that first we understand what *is*
happening: What *is* the reality now?

Second, based on what *is*, we articulate what we *want* to happen.

Finally, by negotiating a compromise between what *is* and what we *want*,
we can arrive at a decision: what *should* be done.

But very often, the actual sequence in making a decision is different: First,
we decide what we *want*. Once we've finalized what we *want*, we proceed to

finalize what we *should* do in light of what we *want*—and we leave what *is* out of the equation, ignoring reality completely.

I suggest that in the Middle East, both sides have been reasoning in the wrong sequence: Both start their reasoning with what they *want*, and in light of that, they decide what they *should* do.

On both sides, *reality* takes a back seat.

The Palestinian Approach

To focus on what one *wants* is typical of a nation—or any other form of organization—at the beginning of its lifecycle. The Palestinians, just like the Jews in the late 19th and early 20th centuries, when Zionism began taking root, are a new nation and think like one: To build a nation, they believe they must start with what they *want*.

When Theodore Herzl, the father of modern Zionism, first began arguing in favor of an independent Jewish state, he famously stated: "If you will it, it is no fairytale"; in other words, if you want it badly enough, you can make it happen. The Palestinians probably have their own slogan that makes the same point.

So, what do the Palestinians *want*? Apparently, they want Israel to give the right of return to millions of descendants of the original Palestinian refugees. They are not particularly interested in the reality, which is that, should Israel allow millions of Palestinians into the country, it would lose its Jewish majority and, by definition, become something other than a Jewish state. If that occurred, the aspirations of the Jewish people to have a country of their own where, at least psychologically, they feel secure, would be defeated.

The Palestinians also want Israel to return to its 1967 borders, which means uprooting hundreds of thousands of Israelis who now live beyond those borders.

There is no leader in Israel who has the CAPI—all the coalesced authority, power, and influence—necessary to implement this solution. Israel is a democratic state; its government, like that of the United States, potentially rises and

> *The reality is that they have to live together. … A Palestinian state will be established, economic collaboration will be agreed on … the Palestinians will learn Hebrew and the Israelis Arabic. … That is the only solution that can work.*

falls with each election. As a result, to remain in power, all Israeli leaders have to walk a very thin line regarding what they can and cannot do.

What the Palestinians *want* will not happen. Six million Israelis are not going to simply disappear one day; they are not going to go back to their ancestors' countries of origin, *or* to the 1967 borders, *or* live in a Palestinian state. The Palestinians could never make the Israelis' lives *so* miserable that they would agree to give the Palestinians what they want. No intifada could be terrible enough to make the Israelis leave the land of Israel. They will adapt to the ubiquitous terror, as we are now watching them do.

THE ISRAELI APPROACH

Jews have more than 2,500 years of experience with persecution; you might say it is an area of expertise. The horrors of World War II are still sharp in their collective memory. Their slogan "Never again" is not just an empty phrase; it is an oath, a promise, to the generations to come.

What do the Israelis *want?* They *want* to be a normal nation, with their own country, where they can protect themselves from the numerous enemies they have encountered over many generations. They want a peace-seeking leadership to emerge among the Palestinians, who will withdraw the refugees' claim to the right of return, who will agree to several adaptations to the 1967 borders (or else accept settlements of militant Israeli settlers in their midst), and who will sign a permanent peace agreement.

In short, this is what Israeli Prime Minister Ehud Barak offered at Camp David in 2000, and it is what most Israelis claim is the most they can offer. (The extreme Israeli right seems to want the Palestinians to be absorbed by the Arab countries that surround Israel, and stop existing as a nation-seeking entity, which, clearly, is not going to happen. The only person in the world who *might* have been powerful enough to make that happen was Yasser Arafat, and he could not—or would not—do it. And now he is dead. It will be a very long time before another Palestinian leader could emerge who is strong enough to do it and yet survive politically.)

Nor is there any chance that the Israelis can make the lives of the Palestinians so miserable that they will get down on their knees and beg to implement the Israeli solution. The more miserable the Palestinians' lives become, the smaller the chance that a peace-seeking leadership will emerge and be able to survive the mob.

Thus this solution, based on what Israel *wants*, is also a dead end.

It is this sequence—of both sides sticking to what they *want* and deciding what *should* be done based on those wants—that is preventing the negotiation of a workable solution.

What either of the parties *wants* is not going to happen, no matter how many people are killed or sacrifice their lives. And if both sides start with a non-negotiable *want*, neither party will be able to do what they *should* do to solve the problem.

Thus, we are left with the *is*: What *is* going to happen? Not what the parties *want,* nor what the parties *should* do. If left to themselves (assuming there is no intervention of external forces, such as the United States forcing Israel to give up land), here is what I predict the dynamics of the system might produce:

It will simply get worse and worse. Both parties will suffer more and more.

The parties will become willing to change their unworkable strategies only when what *is* going on is so terrible that they will be forced to let go of what they *want* and what they think the other side *should* do. Only then will a paradigm shift happen.

WORST-CASE SCENARIO

How bad would that have to be?

I am thinking of a nuclear explosion. Tactical nuclear devices *are* available. The only question is: When will a dissident, uncontrollable group of Palestinians, supported by Osama bin Laden, or Iran, or Pakistan, acquire such a device? At that point, it won't be difficult to recruit a suicide terrorist who, instead of wrapping twenty pounds of explosives around his waist, will carry a nuclear device and detonate it in Tel Aviv or Haifa. If thousands of Arabs perish along with Jews, these fanatics will simply consider it collateral damage. For them, apparently, such damage is not a deterrent; they have already killed many Israeli Arabs by detonating explosives on buses and in mixed Arab-Israeli coffee shops.

Then the Israelis will retaliate. And when hundreds of thousands die—not just twenty here and thirty there—when massive destruction shakes the world to its foundations, only then will a paradigm shift occur, and the sequence of reasoning change from *want/should/is,* to *is/want/should.* The parties will finally be forced to deal with reality.

And the reality is that they *have to* live together. They *are* neighbors, sharing air and water that recognize no man-made boundaries whatsoever. A Palestinian state *will* be established, economic collaboration *will* be agreed on, freedom of movement of labor and goods between the countries *will* be granted, the Palestinians *will* learn Hebrew and the Israelis Arabic, both sides *will* remove all the hateful and disrespectful components from their educational curricula and forbid hatred in their media. That is the only solution that can work.

But so far, neither side is ready to face this reality.

Both live in fear, not with faith. Both are at the beginning of their lifecycles, when typically what people *want* dominates their reasoning. Accepting what *is* comes with maturity—or, unfortunately, after a disaster. That is when people finally let go of what they *want* and look at reality first.

It appears that it takes a major crisis for humans to make a major change in direction. The bigger the change that is needed, the bigger the crisis that has to happen to cause the necessary paradigm shift in thinking and reasoning to occur.

AMERICAN AND ISRAELI STRATEGIES DIVERGE ON IRAN[1]

A hen and a pig were good friends for many years. One day the hen had a great idea:

"Let's open a restaurant and serve an American breakfast of ham and eggs, and make some money," the hen said excitedly.

"Great idea," said the pig, "except that what is only a contribution for you is a total sacrifice for me!"

Despite their friendship, the stakes are not the same for the United States and Israel (or even Europe and Israel) if Iran develops operational nuclear weapons.

On numerous occasions, radical Iranian clerics have expressed their morbid intention to wipe Israel off the map. And who says they won't carry out their threat? Can Israel take a chance and assume they won't? What price would it pay if its assumption turned out to be wrong?

What would the United States do if Al-Qaeda installed missiles with nuclear capability in Cuba and declared its intention to wipe parts of the United States off the map? Offer diplomatic negotiations to resolve the problem?

When you do not have a choice, you do not have a problem to ponder. You just have to act. And Israel has no choice. It has to do something to stop Iran from building a nuclear arsenal.

However, for the United States to attack Iran—to open a third front— the stakes are too high. To be openly belligerent toward Iran, and to support Israeli actions to stop Iran, also has the political cost of further angering radical Muslims.

So, what is the best strategy for the United States?

---

[1] Adizes Insights, August 2009.

Tell the world that it is for diplomacy, for continuing negotiations. Send Secretary of Defense Robert Gates to Israel and have him tell the media that he has strongly suggested to the Israeli leadership that they should have patience and do nothing, etc. But, quietly and secretly, encourage the Israelis to do the dirty job. That way, the United States will appear in the world's opinion polls as peace-loving, while Israel will do what needs to be done.

PUBLIC RELATIONS DISASTER

It's a perfect scenario for the United States, but a public relations disaster for Israel. Once more, Israel will be seen as the aggressor, the uncontrollable bully of the Middle East, the ungrateful ally who rejects the advice of its benefactor and decides to use force, even though the United States claimed there was no need to do so.

What might be the long-term repercussions for Israel of this growing negative image?

Israel already has few friends left among the family of nations. World-wide, the political left wing harbors anti-Israeli sentiment, because it always supports the underdog. Anti-Semites are enjoying endless opportunities to justify their hate. The only supporters Israel has left are radical Christians, who support Israel because, according to the Bible, God promised that land to the Jews. Their support is solid, because God's promise is solid, but how many votes do radical Christians have now? Hasn't their political power waned since George W. Bush left the White House?

The growing anti-Israel talk should have caused Israel to massively increase its strategic public relations. Instead, its advertising continues to aim at luring more tourists to the Holy Land by focusing on bikini-clad young Israeli girls.

Unfortunately, Israel does not seem particularly concerned about anti-Israeli sentiment. Israeli strategic PR is worse than mediocre. They preach to the choir, making their presentations mostly in synagogues.

Why is that? Are they not worried about the rising tide of anti-Israeli attitude?

SO WHAT ELSE IS NEW?

When, years ago, I tried to convince a very senior member of the Israeli Cabinet to invest major resources in strategic PR, he said: "It won't help. They'll hate us anyway." And he was not alone in feeling this way.

For thousands of years, the Jewish people have been rejected, criticized, and hated. So what else is new? Jews just accept rejection and keep going.

But right now, this imperviousness to criticism and hatred is not serving Israel well. Having the whole world turn against Israel would be an alarming development. I can easily imagine not only academic and cultural, but also economic sanctions levied against Israel. And as the radical Christian vote becomes weaker and the left and pro-Arabs stronger, I can imagine even the United States withdrawing its support. If that happens, American Jewry would find itself immobilized, afraid that supporting Israel would raise doubts about its allegiance to America.

Israel *is* in danger—*grave* danger.

It is in a lose-lose situation: Lose if it acts, and lose even more if it does *not* act.

ON FEELING JEWISH[1]
(PART 1 OF 3)

DURING the Yom Kippur prayers, for which I was in Jerusalem this year, I had some thoughts that I would like to share with you.

These thoughts are contained in three separate Insights, to be read in sequence. This is the first.

FRANKFURT, PASSPORT CONTROL

A man in a police uniform sitting at a height above me is checking my passport. I tense up. I wonder: Why am I tense? My passport is legitimate. No visa is necessary. I am not carrying anything illegal. *Why am I tense?*

Then I realize: It is a *German* policeman.

It has been sixty years since I was in a camp. But somehow my body remembers, and reacts.

FLYING TO ISRAEL

I am on my way to Tel Aviv. Boarding is announced. We are taken to a bus and driven away from the gates to a desolate place where the plane is parked, surrounded by policemen with machine guns drawn. Our bus is accompanied by a police car.

I tense up. I realize: There is a threat to my life. There might be a terrorist attack.

I feel persecuted. I feel tense and on guard all the time.

RIGA, LATVIA

I received my thirteenth honorary doctorate from the university there. The next day I took the afternoon off to see the city, and visited the

---

[1] Adizes Insights, October 2009.

synagogue. Above the Holy Ark is written, in Hebrew: "Blessed are you, our Lord, for not giving us as prey to their jaws."

This is unusual. I've never seen this quote in a synagogue. Ever. I ask the shammes, the synagogue attendant, why this particular line from the Old Testament was quoted.

He tells me that of the 70,000 Jews who lived in Riga before the war, only a few remained alive afterward. Those survivors built this synagogue, and are thanking God for surviving.

"Were the others gassed?" I ask.

"They did not have to be," says the shammes. "Latvia is 50 percent forest. They took them there, men, women, and children, all families, murdered them, and put them in mass graves.

"About forty women and their children hid in the synagogue, hoping that the sacred place would give them refuge. The Nazis poured gasoline on the synagogue walls and burned them all alive."

I can't hold back my tears. I feel embarrassed in front of my hosts: Just the day before they had honored me in a ceremony with an honorary doctorate, and now, I am not in control of my body's reaction.

KIEV

In Kiev, there is a large sculpture of Bogdan Khmel-nitsky, a leader of the Ukrainian independence movement, but also *oher Israel* (an enemy of the Jews), who led many pogroms. Again I tense up.

My wife's family owns a piece of a Torah parchment that has been passed down from one generation to the next. In the middle of the parchment is a large red blot—the blood of Jews who were murdered during the Kishinev pogrom in 1903.

Above the Holy Ark is written, in Hebrew:"Blessed are you, our Lord, for not giving us as prey to their jaws."

INHERITED MEMORIES

I am reading a book about the Jewish people during the Spanish Inquisition. Since I am a Sephardic Jew, it was my ancestors who were tortured at that time. As I read the book, I notice that I am sweating.

It seems that our genes do not transfer only physical characteristics and personality traits; it seems to me that they also transfer traumatic memories.

A friend of mine once questioned whether it was worth remaining Jewish. "Why the suffering? Enough is enough," he said.

I believe that he can change whom he serves, how he prays, where he prays, and if he prays at all, but he cannot escape being Jewish as long as the cells in his body remember what it means to be Jewish.

In the Israeli newspapers, I read of an American professor, whose field of research is post-traumatic stress disorder, who reports longitudinal research indicating that Israeli society is exhibiting post-traumatic behavior. This doesn't surprise me. The Holocaust experience is with me, in my cells, in my sweat. ...

Sanctuary

I am watching the Animal Planet Channel on television. The program is about a rare breed of sea lions that is becoming extinct. They have been given a sanctuary, an island off the coast of Mexico, and no one is allowed to disturb them or hunt them. Other animals that used to be on that island have been transferred to give those sea lions a chance to survive.

> It seems that our genes do not transfer only physical characteristics and personality traits; it seems to me that they also transfer traumatic memories.

Oh God, I say to myself. Why whales and sea lions, yes, but the Jews, no? We have been hunted, burned, gassed, maimed, for generations. There is no one in Israel who cannot name at least one family member who was murdered because he was a Jew. In my extended family alone, I count 103 members, including my grandparents, who were gassed in Treblinka.

Why can't the United Nations proclaim that the Jews are a nation in danger of becoming extinct (we are only thirteen million worldwide), and let us live in peace in Israel, the homeland of the Jewish people, a tiny piece of land, 63 percent of which is desert. Why can they not prosecute anyone who tries to murder us, such as Iranian President Mahmoud Ahmadinejad, who claims the Holocaust did not happen and frequently announces that he intends to wipe the Jewish homeland, and everyone in it, "off the map."

And his threat is not an empty one. He is working diligently on developing a nuclear bomb.

"But Jews are strong," I hear people say. "They rule the world. They don't need protection. *We* need protection from *them*. They are too strong and rich and smart, etc…"

If we are so strong and smart, why can't we prevent ourselves being attacked and murdered in every generation?

When will this persecution end? When will my body stop tensing up? Will my children always be tense, too? And my grandchildren?

Will we Jews ever find peace? When will the world finally recognize our right to have peace, the right to survive?

CAN ISRAEL DO BETTER?[1]
(PART 2 OF 3)

ZIONISM defines Israel as a Jewish state, a refuge for Jews who are threatened anywhere in the world. Thus, any Jew, wherever in the world she is born, has an automatic right to Israeli citizenship.

After 2,500 years of persecution and the horrors of the Holocaust, this vision of Israel as a sanctuary is natural and definitely justifiable. But what are its repercussions?

We have a Jewish state, in which the Arab minority (by definition not Jewish) is treated as a foreign element. A newly arriving Jew has rights not granted to an Arab born in Israel, even if his ancestors were born there.

Israel, with its Western culture, is a small island in a sea of more than a quarter billion Muslims, most of whom reject Western values and feel threatened by them. Thus, Israel is perceived as a colonizer, usurping Arab land by force, viewing its most recent inhabitants as second-class citizens, and being itself viewed as an outpost of values that threaten traditional Muslim culture.

It should come as no surprise that the Muslim world would love to eject this foreign body and eliminate Israel's existence altogether.

Of course, Israel continues to do whatever it must to defend itself from those repetitive hostile and potentially fatal efforts. That has meant an ongoing state of war. And wars are never simple, easy, or clean; inevitably, there are civilian deaths and violations of human rights.

But Israel's behavior has not been worse than the United States' behavior in Vietnam and, more recently, in Iraq. The same can be said of the French in Algiers and the Allied forces during World War II.

Has the United Nations appointed a committee to analyze *their* possible crimes against humanity? Never. But it has repeatedly investigated Israel,

---

[1] Adizes Insights, October 2009.

providing fodder to anti-Semites who need very little encouragement to attack Israel on any front.

Since people generally equate Israelis and Jews, Israel's actions during its numerous wars and its treatment of the Arabs feed anti-Semitism world-wide. This means that in effect, Israel, instead of protecting the world's Jews, is now threatening their peace in the Diaspora.

Israelis aren't particularly sympathetic to this argument. "So they should all make *aliya* [immigrate to Israel]," they respond.

But is that the best solution? The Jewish sage Rashi once asked himself why God had seen fit to spread the Jews all over the globe. The answer, he concluded, was so that the enemies of the Jews "cannot destroy us easily by finding us all in one place."

Are we less vulnerable in Israel? Or, on the contrary, are we sitting ducks? And how do we stop—or at least reduce—the continual negative press that is affecting the Jewish Diaspora?

WHAT TO DO?

Israel needs to make more of an effort to be part of the Middle East, more of an integrating force.

What is realistically possible? Could Israel give its Arab population totally equal rights regarding where they can live and work? Not yet. Realistically, that is inconceivable as long as terrorism is a way of life in Israel.

Stop the wars? We all wish for this, but that wish—which would require a peace settlement—has not been granted and cannot be granted by one side unilaterally.

Conduct more humane wars? I honestly believe the Israeli army is as humane as it is possible to be. But wars are wars, especially when the enemy operates out of hospitals and schools.

> Israel, with its Western culture, is a small island in a sea of more than a quarter billion Muslims, most of whom reject Western values and feel threatened by them.

The past is usually a pretty good predictor of the future. But we know that in life, situations either get better or they get worse, and the rule of entropy teaches us that unless we make it better, it will become worse by default.

While economic conditions in Israel have improved immensely over the years, its relations with its own Arab population have only become worse.

Israel can do better. Not everything is impossible. For instance, it could change the educational system to require that every high school graduate be fluent in three languages: Hebrew, Arabic, and English.

It should teach not only Jewish philosophy in its schools, but also Muslim philosophy. It should have more joint ventures with the Arab population.

These changes might not be enough to change the picture, but at least they will be steps in the right direction if Israel wants to be part of the Middle East, instead of a European satellite country that happens to be located in the Middle East.

QUO VADIS, ZIONISM?[1]
(PART 3 OF 3)

I am afraid this Insight will make me persona non grata in Israel, the country I love with all my heart.

I am already in trouble in my birth country, Macedonia, where I dared to challenge the government for not settling its name dispute with Greece. The Macedonian prime minister actually took the time to denounce me on television.

But I believe in the motto of *Ha Olam Haze* magazine: "without fear or pretense." So allow me to say what is bothering me, and if someone can convince me that I am wrong, I will be the first to admit it publicly.

What is it that is eating me up?

Zionism, the movement to create a national Jewish homeland in Israel, was born out of the infamous anti-Semitic Dreyfus trial in 1890s France. Journalist Theodore Herzl, while covering that trial, concluded and began to persuade others that the only way Jews could stop being the world's oddballs and misfits was to return to their homeland, Israel, and become *ke kol ha amim*, a normal country like all other countries.

This expression—*ke kol ha amim*—haunts me.

Why?

Because, ironically, every Jewish prayer contains a sentence thanking God for *not* making us *ke goyey ha adama*, like the rest of the world.

We are the "chosen people," whose role is to be *or la goyeem*, a light to the world.

So what happened when we tried being like the rest of the world? We succeeded. Now we have an army and we rely on force rather than on spirit to solve our problems, even though it is precisely our spirit—our values system,

---

[1] Adizes Insights, October 2009.

mutual help, and over-developed, almost exaggerated conscience—that has distinguished the Jewish people for thousands of years. *Ruah* (spirit), rather than *koah* (force).

Today, Israel is no different from any other country. We have poverty. We have hungry children. We have Jewish prostitutes and Jewish robbers. Our system of education is deteriorating rapidly; what was once the crown jewel of Jewish culture, education, is being devalued and lost.

In other words, we are now "normal."

Is that what we want? To be "normal"?

Zionists would like every Jew in the world to immigrate to Israel and be "normal." But is that really our destiny? Is that our shared vision of Judaism? Should it be? What happened to the vision of being *or la goyeem*—providing moral benchmarks, acting as the whole world's canary in the coal mine of consciousness?

In short, what happened to being special, different—"chosen"?

THE DANGERS OF SECULARIZATION

Another thing that bothers me: Secular Israelis behave differently from secular Jews anywhere else in the world.

They have a country, an army, and they supposedly feel secure— "normal"—while other Jews, wherever they reside, are supposedly still a foreign body and thus "abnormal."

But for Jews who became Israelis, "normal" not only conveyed a sense of security, it also legitimized being secular. A secular Zionist—i.e., secular Israeli—can still be a Jew, and a proud one, without feeling guilt for not practicing the religious rituals. He is Jewish by default, simply by being Israeli.

That is not how a Jew in the Diaspora feels. If a Diaspora Jew does not practice the religion, or practices only some of the time, he doubts the authenticity, or at least the quality, of his Judaism.

With the establishment of the state of Israel, secular Zionism had the unintended effect of bifurcating nationality from religion: You could be a Jewish national—a secular Israeli—without sharing or practicing the religion.

In the United States, I have often seen secular Israelis ignore Judaism's holiest days, openly holding a barbecue on Yom Kippur and eating "white steaks" (pig meat) publicly.

Secular Israelis rarely, if ever, go to a synagogue. They feel Israeli first, second, and third. Jewish? Yes, but a different kind of Jewish. Or, as someone in Israel once quipped: "They are goyim who speak Hebrew."

Israelis do not identify with world Jewry. When they emigrate from Israel, often they do not mix with the Jewish community in their new country. They are out of touch with the Reform way of practicing religion (schoolchildren in Israel are taught to ridicule Reform Jews for their compromises with Orthodox practice), but they have no idea how to practice the Orthodox or even the Conservative way, because they have never learned it.

Take me, for instance. I never learned any of the Jewish prayers or rituals when I was growing up in Israel. So whenever I find myself in a synagogue, anywhere in the world, I feel lost, alien; I have a painful sense that I don't belong.

Secular Zionism has cut the chain that connected Jews for many generations. Young, non-religious Israelis have no religious roots and thus are alien to the Jewish community worldwide, and vice versa.

Efforts to bring young Jewish people from around the world to visit Israel and stay for a while are based on the assumption that this strengthens their bond to Judaism. I disagree. Such trips may encourage them to make *aliya* (immigrate to Israel). But why would they make young people feel more connected to *Judaism*? On the contrary, in Israel they discover a new way of being a Jew without being Jewish.

I repeat for emphasis: If you are Israeli, you do not have to be "Jewish" to be a Jew.

But what would happen if the state of Israel, God forbid, ceased to exist? Scattered to the winds again without a homeland, would the surviving secular Israelis revert to the religious traditions that once helped bind the Jewish people, or would they give up being Jewish altogether?

Could we survive as secular Israeli Jews without our land—and if so, for how long?

WAS HERZL A FALSE MESSIAH?

In 1970, I saw a play by Yosef Mundy called *It Turns*, which still haunts me today. In it, Theodore Herzl, the founder of Zionism and "father" of the state of Israel, is accused of being a "false messiah," like Sabbatai Zevi.

In 18th-century Turkey, Sabbatai Zevi proclaimed himself to be the Messiah; thousands followed him, believing he would bring redemption to the Jewish people. Later, however, under threat to his life, he converted to Islam, inducing many of his followers to do the same. He cost the Jewish community thousands of conversions, and was ultimately declared to be a false messiah.

> Secular Zionism has cut the chain that connected Jews for many generations.

In the play, Herzl is asked, "Are you, too, a false messiah?" I wonder. If so, the consequences of the movement he founded could be *millions* of Jews lost to religious Judaism—and thus each other—despite all its richly detailed rites and close families.

Do we care? Should we do something? Is it time to redefine our mission?

I do not think we can answer this question by reversing the wheels of history and challenging Israel's right to exist for the Jewish people. There is no way back to the horrible past—and for that I am grateful.

Israel must exist for the Jewish people, who should have a country of their own, as all nations aim to have. The question is not why or what, but how. Here are some thoughts, just to start the discussion.

ZIONISM FOR THE 21ST CENTURY

Point 1: Israel has to return to its roots, back to its religious foundation, and teach Judaism with all the rituals from nursery school up. It is essential that we reconnect with world Jewry, and the way to do that is through our shared religion. What unites us with world Jewry is our religion, not the Jewish nationalism that Zionism promotes.

Please note that by "religion" I do not necessarily mean Orthodox practice. Since world Jewry practices its religion in multiple ways, so should the Israelis. For various reasons, most secular Jews have rejected Orthodoxy; thus, the current Orthodox monopoly in Israel over what it means to practice Judaism has alienated millions of born Jews from their own religion.

All Jews worldwide need to be able to pray together, to share a sense of being responsible for one another, and to share our commitment to *tikkun olam* (making the world a better place).

Point 2: Zionists can also be those who do not choose to live in Israel. To be a Zionist, one need only actively support the principle that a Jewish state *should* exist, and that any Jew who wants to live there can.

Point 3: We need to start the discussion of how to redefine Zionism for the 21st century. What role should Israel play in the future of the Jewish people? How much added value does Israel offer—and at the same time, what liabilities does it bring to the table?

Let us get on with it.

ABOUT THE ADIZES INSTITUTE

For the past 35 years, the Adizes Institute has been committed to equipping visionary leaders, management teams, and agents of change to become champions of their industries and markets. These leaders have successfully established a collaborative organizational culture by using Adizes' pragmatic tools and concepts to achieve peak performance.

Adizes specializes in guiding leaders of organizations (CEOs, top management teams, boards, owners) to quickly and effectively resolve issues such as:

- Difficulties in executing good decisions.
- Making the transition from entrepreneurship to professional management.
- Difficulties in aligning the structure of the organization to achieve its strategic intent.
- "Bureaucratizing": when an organization gets out of touch with its markets and begins to lose entrepreneurial vitality.
- Conflicts among founders, owners, board members, partners, and family members.
- Internal management team conflicts and "politics" severe enough to inhibit the success of the business.
- Growing pains.
- Culture clashes between companies undergoing mergers or acquisitions.

Adizes also offers comprehensive training and certification for change leaders who wish to incorporate into their practice the Adizes methodologies for managing change.

Adizes is the primary sponsor of the Adizes Graduate School, a nonprofit teaching organization that offers Master's and Ph.D. programs for the Study of Leadership and Change.

For more information about these and other programs,
please visit www.adizes.com.